1987

Theater Games For The Classroom

A Teacher's Handbook

Viola Spolin

Theater Games For The Classroom

A Teacher's Handbook

Viola Spolin

Edited by
Arthur Morey
Mary Ann Brandt

Northwestern
University
Press

Evanston, Illinois
1986

CONTENTS

In memory of
Neva L. Boyd,
who loved the children.

Viola Spolin began her work with children in 1924, as a student at Neva Boyd's school of creative drama, and then as drama supervisor for Chicago's WPA Recreational Project. There, she began to evolve simple exercises to solve the complicated problems that arise in children's theater.

In 1946, Mrs. Spolin founded and directed the Young Actors Company in Hollywood. Here, she used her games to train children for formal dramatic productions. In 1955, she returned to Chicago to run workshops for the country's first improvisational acting company. Her work with her son Paul Sills in the formation of Second City laid the foundation for all improvisational companies since.

In 1963, she published *Improvisation for the Theater*, which made her techniques accessible for the first time not only to theater groups, but also to the classroom drama teacher. Twenty-three years later, it remains a best seller in drama bookstores and with teachers alike. Over 100,000 copies are now in print in English and the book has been translated into German, Dutch, and Portuguese.

Following publication of *Improvisation for the Theater*, Spolin co-founded the Game Theater in Chicago, was asked to present her games to a gathering of the National Council for English Teachers, and taught at Brandeis University. In 1975, she founded the Spolin Theater Games Center in Los Angeles.

The Secondary School Theater Association awarded Mrs. Spolin its Founders Award in 1976. In 1978, she received an honorary Doctor of Arts degree from Eastern Michigan University. In 1983, the Children's Theater Association presented her its Monte Meacham Award for life-time acheivement. In 1985, she received commendations from President Ronald Reagan, the Governor of California, and the Los Angeles City Council for her work.

☐ *Books by Spolin:*

Improvisation for the Theater *(1963)*
(Northwestern University Press)

A Directors Handbook *(1985)*
(Northwestern University Press)

PREFACE

The games in this book are exercises designed for teachers of diverse backgrounds. But, although they are accessible to students and teachers alike, the games have a very serious intent. They help students in developing performance skills and lead them to an understanding of what it is to be an artist. The writer intends, that is, not merely to provide students with theater experiences but to help them become responsive to their fellow players, able to create an environment through behavior and to transform ordinary objects into extraordinary ones. Most important, the games will make students more knowledgeable about themselves. Playing theater games, students will learn not only a variety of performance skills but the basic rules of storytelling, literary criticism, and character analysis. Through play, they will develop imagination and intuition; they will find it easier to project themselves into unfamiliar situations. And, by being exposed to their own creative and artistic possibilities, they will, of necessity, learn to concentrate their energies, to share what they know. These games, in short, go beyond the theatrical to nurture skills and attitudes that are useful in every aspect of learning and life.

— A.M.

Chapter 1:
WHY BRING THEATER GAMES INTO THE CLASSROOM?

Designed for the teacher who has had little or no training in the theater, this book is a step-by-step guide to the organization of theater-game workshops in the classroom. The theater workshop can become a place where teachers and students meet as fellow players, involved with one another, ready to connect, to communicate, to experience, to respond, and to experiment and discover.

Playing theater games with your students will bring refreshment, vitality, and more. Theater-game workshops are designed not as diversions from the curriculum, but rather as supplements, increasing student awareness of problems and ideas fundamental to their intellectual development. Many of the games contain notes connecting them with a variety of study areas. (See Appendix 2 and Index B in Appendix 4.)

Theater-game workshops are useful in improving students' ability to communicate through speech and writing and in nonverbal ways as well. They are energy sources, helping students develop skills in concentration, problem solving, and group interaction.

Games

Years ago when challenged to train students (ages five through teens) in theater techniques, this writer turned to a problem-solving approach, based on the structure of games and exercises, which allowed students to absorb theater skills naturally without conscious effort. Over the years, more than two hundred games and exercises have been designed to stimulate action, relation, spontaneity, and creativity of individuals in a group setting. Students learned by doing, through first-hand experience, rather than by lectures in ready-made formulas. This play-oriented workshop approach became the basis for a whole new American branch of theater, blossoming into thousands of improvisational theater groups around the country.

☐ *A game is a set of rules that a player decides to live within. The rules don't so much restrict the player as they keep the player playing.*
☐ *Acting is doing.*

☐ *"Many children, young people and adults can enjoy the experience of dramatic art within the confines of the workshop environment without the need or desire to extend that experience into public performance."*
— *Margaret Faulkes*

Play

In play, the skills and strategies necessary to the game are developed. Ingenuity and inventiveness meet any crises the game presents, for it is understood that all participants are free to reach the game's objective in any manner they choose. As long as they abide by the rules of the game, players may stand on their heads or fly through the air. In fact, any unusual or extraordinary way of resolving the problem of the game is likely to be applauded by one's fellow players.

Many of the skills learned in playing are social skills. Most games worth playing are highly social and have a problem that needs solving within them — an objective point in which each individual must become involved with others while attempting to reach a goal.

Outside of play there are few places where children can contribute to the world in which they find themselves. Their world, controlled by adults who tell them what to do and when to do it, offers them little opportunity to act or to accept community responsibility. The theater-game workshop is designed to offer students the opportunity for equal freedom, respect, and responsibility within the community of the schoolroom.

☐ *Play is democratic! Anyone can play! Everyone can learn through playing! Play touches and stimulates vitality, awakening the whole person — mind and body, intelligence and creativity, spontaneity and intuition — when all, teacher and students together, are attentive to the moment.*

Freedom

But a child can make an honest and exciting contribution to the classroom theater workshop only if allowed the personal freedom to play the games. The player must be free to interact with, to experience, his or her social and physical environment. Young players can accept responsibility for communication; can become involved; can develop relationships and learn to improve and to evolve theatrically valid scenes, but only when given the freedom to do so.

☐ *When the student actor responds joyfully, effortlessly, the teacher/director will know that the theater is in his or her very bones.*

Intuition

Experience comes from direct contact with the environment, total organic involvement with it. This means involvement on all levels: intellectual, physical, and intuitive. The intuition, most vital to learning, is most often neglected. Intuition is often thought to be an endowment or a mystical force enjoyed by the gifted alone, yet all of us have known moments when the right answer "just came" or we did "exactly the right thing without thinking." Sometimes at such moments, usually precipitated by crisis, danger, or shock, "average" people have been known to transcend the limitations of the familiar, to enter courageously the area of the unknown, and to experience the release of momentary genius within themselves. The intuitive can only be felt in the moment of spontaneity, the moment when we are freed to relate and act, involving ourselves in the moving, changing world around us.

☐ *Intuition bypasses the intellect, the mind, the memory, the known. Using intuition cannot be taught. One must be tripped into it.*

☐ *There is, clearly, a strong resemblance between improvisation in the theater and jazz. Art Farmer, the jazz flugelhorn player, says, "You can never force what you're doing. The harder you try, the less happens. At the best times, it's as if you had been taken over by some other power. This power plays you, and you become the instrument."*

Transformation

The effects of game playing are not only social and cognitive. When players are deeply focused on a game, they are capable of transforming objects or creating them. Whole environments arise spontaneously out of thin air. Impossible to capture fully in words, transformations seem to arise out of heightened physical movement and of exchange of this moving energy between players. Change occurs not once but over and over again.

Transformations are theater magic and an intrinsic part of most theater games.

☐ *The heart of improvisation is transformation.*

☐ *Creativity is not rearranging; it is transformation.*

Three Essentials of a Theater Game

Special attention is given here to focus, sidecoaching, and evaluation — three essential parts of any theater game.

Focus

Each game's stated focus is a problem that is essential to the playing that can be solved by the players. In workshops, the teacher will present the focus as part of the game, strive to keep himself or herself attentive to that focus while sidecoaching players as necessary toward the same end. The focus sets the game in motion. All become fellow players as they attend to the same problem from different points of view. With focus between all, dignity and privacy are maintained and true peerage can evolve. Trust the focus. Let it work for you.

The focus is *not* the objective of the game in and of itself. Trying to stay on focus generates the energy needed for playing which is then channeled and flows through the given structure of the game to shape the event. The effort to stay on focus and the uncertainty about outcome diminish prejudices, create mutual support, and generate organic involvement in the playing. All, teacher (sidecoach) and students (players), are tripped into the present moment, alerted to solve the problem. As an eight-year-old player very aptly once said, "It takes all your strength to stay on focus."

Trust the focus in the games and watch it spill over into daily routines. Keep everyone playing and discover the hidden creativity in those whose usual classroom performance is unsatisfactory. Be patient. Soon you will find your least responsible children taking justifiable pride in what they do.

Sidecoaching

Sidecoaching is the calling out of just that word, that phrase, or that sentence that keeps the player on focus. Sidecoaching phrases arise spontaneously out of what is emerging in the playing area and are given at the time players are in movement. Sidecoaching must guide players toward focus, creating interaction, movement, and transformation. (Sidecoaching for the games is printed in bold italics in the right-hand, narrow column: ***Show! Don't tell!***)

□ *"The [Spolin theater games] are artifices agains artificiality, structures designed to almost fool spontaneity into being — or perhaps a frame carefully built to keep out interferences in which the player waits. Important in the game is the "ball" — the Focus, a technical problem, sometimes a double technical problem which keeps the mind (a censoring device) so busy rubbing its stomach and its head in opposite directions, so to speak, that genius (spontaneity), unguarded, happens."*
— Film Quarterly

□ *Watch for excessive activity in the early sessions of workshops; discourage all performing, all cleverness. Keep everyone's attention on focus at all times. This discipline will bring the timid ones to fuller awareness and channel the freer ones towards greater personal development.*

□ *Learn by doing. The concepts behind theater games are much clearer once you have begun playing.*

Sidecoaching holds players to focus whenever they may have wandered away. (**Keep your eye on the ball!**) This keeps each player within the activity and close to a moment of fresh experience. Further, it gives the teacher/director his or her place within the game as a fellow player.

All but a few games include suggested sidecoaching. At first, use the given sidecoaching phrases, calling them out during play at appropriate moments. Later you will discover the proper coaching without following the text. Groups and individuals differ in personal response. Sidecoaching can be evocative, resourceful; it can be a stimulating, provoking, coaxing catalyst. Additions to the printed coaching will come spontaneously and instantaneously to you when you yourself are working on or toward focus.

Try to avoid a barrage of pointless directions. Wait for the emerging play. Remember you too are a player. To sidecoach effectively, use a simple, direct calling out: **Share the stage picture! Keep it in the space — out of your head! Share your voice! Help your fellow player who isn't playing!** When sidecoaching is given as part of the process, players respond freely.

In early work with your students, many of them, because they are used to giving you their attention when you speak, may stop playing to look at you when you sidecoach. This is a sign that they are not accepting you as a fellow player as yet. Try sidecoaching the following: **Listen to my voice but keep right on going!**

Sidecoaching is general, not directed at individual players, and seeks basically to keep all players (including the audience players) on focus. Avoid use of images during sidecoaching. (That is, don't ask players to imagine or pretend something.) Suggesting images to players imposes past thoughts upon what is happening now. Sidecoaching should not alter the course of playing but simply strive to keep all players and the sidecoach, too, on focus.

Evaluation

Evaluation is nonjudgmental. It is not critical, but, like sidecoaching, grows out of the focus. Evaluation questions listed in the games are often a restatement of the focus. They deal with the problems the focus poses and ask whether or not the problems have been solved. (Evaluation for the games is printed in regular italics in the

☐ *Sidecoaching alters the traditional relationship of teacher and student, creating a moving relation. It allows the teacher/director an opportunity to step into the excitement of playing (learning) in the same space, with the same focus as the players.*

☐ *Remember that a player can only take chances when he or she trusts the games, the group, the sidecoach. There are no rewards for winning; in fact, there is no way to win a game. Trust will develop through group evaluations, and initiative will be sparked by sidecoaching.*

☐ *Strive constantly during Evaluation to ask the questions that will meet the experience levels of the children and stimulate their learning.*

narrow, right-hand column, below sidecoaching.)

When one theater-game player or team works on the focus of a game, all other players become audience players viewing the playing. What was communicated or perceived by the audience players is then discussed by all during the evaluation.

In a free environment, asking onstage players, *Do you agree with audience players?* gives them an equal opportunity to take a position on what they have just done. Evaluation often tempts teacher and players alike to dispense their own opinions about the "right way" of doing something. Assume nothing; evaluate only what you have just seen.

The fallacy in the view that there are prescribed ways of behavior came home quite forcibly to this writer one day when a group of players was doing a family scene. Mother, father, grandfather were sitting on a couch, having a tea party. The player showed us he was a grandfather by occasionally saying, "By cracky!" Then, in typical six-year-old fashion, he would climb up and around the couch.

In the evaluation, Johnny was told that he certainly showed us that he was the grandfather. He was then asked by the teacher/director if he thought older men climb around the couch that way. Johnny was startled to hear that he had. Because of the way the questioning was put, Johnny shaped his thinking to meet the teacher/director's frame of reference and then and there accepted her authority and decided, too, that grandfathers do not climb on couches. Suddenly one of the audience players spoke up.

"My grandfather does!"

"He does?"

"Sure, every time he's chasing the cat."

As leaders, we must strive to turn all players, including ourselves, away from personal history back to the present focus of the game. And, while it may be true that only one grandfather out of twenty thousand will climb around couches as does a six-year-old boy, it is a reality that is possible and therefore the player has the right to explore it.

There is no one so dogmatic as the six- or seven-year-old who "knows" the answer. He or she is already reflecting and accepting the patterns of the world. He or she is right and everybody else is wrong! It seems almost impossible at first to eradicate these judgmental and limiting words from the vocabulary of some very young children.

"He's wrong!" a child will say.

"What do you mean by wrong?"

"He didn't do it right."

"What do you mean by right?"

"Like this!" (demonstrating his way to eat cereal).

"What if Johnny wants to do it his way?"

"He's wrong."

"Did you see Johnny eat the cereal?"

"Yes."

"Why was it wrong?"

"He ate it too fast."

"You mean he didn't eat his cereal the way you eat it?"

"You have to eat cereal slowly."

"Who told you that?"

"My mother."

"Well, if your mother wants you to eat cereal slowly, that is the rule of your house. Maybe the rule in Johnny's house is different. Did you see Johnny eat the cereal?"

"Yes."

If one keeps at it, individual differences are finally accepted. Since the cereal Johnny was eating was not actually material in nature, the audience player's admission that it was visible functions to defuse the objection. Be alerted as to when you are passing on a cultural position instead of viewing an actual experience. The words "right," "wrong," "good," "bad" will finally give way to "I didn't see what he was doing." "She didn't move like a doll all of the time." "They didn't share their voices with us."

Approval/Disapproval

We are after direct experience in these workshops.

As leaders and teachers, we should realize that none of us is entirely free from the need to give and receive approval and disapproval. However, having to look to others to tell us where we are, who we are, and what is happening results in a serious loss of personal experiencing. Trying to save ourselves from attack (disapproval) we build a mighty fortress and are timid, or we fight each time we venture forth. Some, in striving for approval, develop egocentricity and exhibitionism; some give up and simply go along. Trying to be "good" or avoiding "being bad" because one can't be "good" can develop into a way of life for those needing approval/disapproval from authority. And the investigation and solving of problems becomes of secondary importance. Passivity is a response to authoritarianism, a giving up of personal responsibility. Playing in workshops should help those who are passive to trust themselves and others to make decisions, to take initiatives, even risks, and to seek freedom.

During theater-game workshops, try to be aware of the effects of approval/disapproval on yourself and your students. When evaluation questions are based on whether the problem (focus) was solved or not and no player is ridiculed, put down, or coyly manipulated, trust in fellow players grows. A peer group is formed and all are freed to take responsibility for their part of playing the game.

☐ *Dependency upon authority obstructs players from directly experiencing self and the world.*

☐ *When we are conditioned to look to others before we can respond, a time-lag is established, a space, a gap, between query and response, which allows the approval/disapproval syndrome to show itself. There is no integrity, no honesty in the reaction of someone debating, "Should I or shouldn't I?"*

☐ *There is no right or wrong way to solve a workshop problem; the honest attempt, the seeking, is what is important.*

☐ *Flattery distracts students from problem solving. They aim for a pat on the head instead of a solution.*

The Game Format

Each game is presented in a recipe-like fashion so it can be read and understood with ease. Following is a typical game with a key to format and use.

Note that many games have variations. Each solves a different problem for the student. Every teacher will find that he or she will invent many additions going through the work.

☐ *Think of each "purpose" as a beginning leading to another beginning.*

Purpose: defines the main result a teacher hopes to get from each game. All games have many uses. But teachers can resolve particular problems that arise in class by consulting **Purpose.**

Focus: The student/player keeps the mind's eye on the **Focus** as a ballplayer keeps his/her eye on the moving ball. **Focus** guarantees involvement of all participants in every moment during the process of playing.

Sidecoaching: (bold italics) is the link between teacher/coach and the students/players. The phrases are assists given *while the game is being played.*

➡

—— ADD A PART ——————————

Purpose: To help players work together in dealing with a large and complicated space object.

Focus: On using part of a whole object in space — out of the head.

Description: Eight to ten players per team. First player uses or makes contact with part of a larger object that only he or she has in mind and then leaves the playing area. One by one, players use or contact other parts of the whole object until the whole object is left in space.

Notes: 1. This game is similar to PART OF A WHOLE, OBJECT, but players do not become the part with their bodies; rather they use parts of a larger space object in the playing area.

2. All stage actors know that, up close, sets are rarely what they seem. They may look like real rooms from the point of view of the audience, but looking downstage one can see that the cabinets have no interiors, the brickwork is styrofoam, the props are papier-mâché.

Let us see what you see!
Give the part its place in space!
Stay with the same whole object!
Other players see the whole through the parts left by others!
Avoid planning your part!
Use what was left by others and let your own part appear!

Audience, what was the complete object?
Were the added parts in the space or in the players' heads?
Players, do you agree?
First player, was that the object you had in mind?

➡

Description: tells the teacher how to organize the game, where to position the players, when to start sidecoaching, when to stop play, etc.

Notes: include observations on what makes the game work most effectively, what difficulties may arise in play and how to solve them, what opportunities to look for, what other games are related, etc.

Evaluation: (light italics) consists of questions for both the students/players and observers. The evaluation reveals what was perceived, learned and/or accomplished in the course of the game.

The Theater-Game Workshop

A workshop is a sequence of activities with a theater game or group of theater games at its core. Each session has a beginning, a middle, and an end. Warm-up games and/or lead-in games prepare players for the day's offerings of theater games, and wrap-up games (like warm-ups) bring players together as a group and help focus energies for the next learning experience.

If possible, make a regular time in your weekly schedule for theater-game workshops. One theater game chosen from the following pages, with its warm-up and lead-in games, can form the framework for a workshop session. How much time is needed to play a specific game or exercise can vary widely depending upon the experience, age, interest, and energy of the group. A young group may take twenty minutes to absorb and enjoy a game that an older group will grasp in five minutes. You, the classroom teacher, the diagnostician, will discover the best solution to this time problem within your own experience of your group.

☐ *Do not rush players. Try always to keep an environment in which each can work according to his or her own nature. An inflexible approach can block growth. In short, don't* teach. *Instead, expose students to the theatrical environment and they will find their own way. Teaching theater to children is much the same as directing adult actors. The differences are ones of presentation. In the classroom, questions and introductions to exercises must be phrased with a clear recognition of the life experiences of children. (Note that sidecoaching directives and evaluation questions in this book have been written at a grade-appropriate level.)*

Workshop Atmosphere

Each theater game workshop should leave you and your students refreshed. However, recognizing the students' right to experiment in approaching a problem puts a burden on the teacher. This way of teaching seems more difficult at first, for you must wait for your students to make discoveries without interpreting or forcing conclusions on them. Only when it becomes clear to individual players that no question will be asked that cannot be answered, no problem given that cannot be solved, can they let go and begin to experiment and experience.

☐ *It is important that the teacher become a fellow player. Do not worry that you may lose your control, your position. Allow the games to do the work. When students feel they "did it themselves," the teacher has succeeded.*

Control

No classroom teacher wants to lose control of the group, and the freedom inherent in improvisational theater games may heighten some teachers' fear of disorder. In practice, as noted elsewhere, players are kept in check by attention to the focus of each game and by the peer pressure that comes from playing in teams. They are not forced to be orderly, they choose order.

☐ *Self-discipline will develop in students when their involvement in the activity is complete.*

Creative freedom does not mean doing away with discipline. It is implicit in true creativity that a free person working in any art form must be highly disciplined. But discipline imposed from above often simply produces inhibited or rebellious action in the student; it can be negative and ineffective. On the other hand, when discipline is not an emotional tug-of-war for position but is freely chosen by the student for the sake of activity, it elicits responsible action — creative action. It takes imagination, dedication, and enthusiasm to be self-disciplined.

□ *The playing of theater games encourages artistic discipline and, by tying the individual to the group, produces responsible personal behavior.*

Energy

When this text calls for you to raise and/or maintain high energy levels, you may feel apprehensive about resulting disorder. But high energy pulls your students together into one community, dissolves lassitude and boredom, promotes interest and focus in the on-going event or project.

If, however, during workshop sessions, students become restless and too undisciplined in their work, this is a danger sign. Refreshment and a new focus are needed. End whatever you are doing immediately and use some simple, quieter game that can involve everyone. Use anything that will bring the group together again through involvement in an activity rather than through admonition or discipline. It's more fun that way. Allow the theater games to do the controlling for you.

□ *Do not confuse the freedom of a theater-game workshop with license. The theater is a highly disciplined art form. Neither expect too much of children nor too little. Self-discipline will evolve in students when their involvement in the activity is complete.*

Day's Order

Come to the workshop with a day's order or plan that includes five to ten games. (That is probably twice the number you will actually play in a session.) Interest, energy, and enthusiasm (or their absence) may require dropping one game and substituting another at a moment's notice. An example of a day's order follows. Games circled were actually played. Numbers indicate the order in which they were played. You may wish to return to the games that were not done in a following session (though it is advisable to begin with a new warm-up game). But if the list for a particular session is not working for you, go on to another.

□ *Most sessions begin and end with a traditional game played as warm-up or wrap-up.*

```
Workshop #5
Sequence #1          Oct. 7, 1987      45 minutes

22 Players           Fourth grade

Traditional Games              Theater Games

EXPLOSION TAG            2. (DODGE BALL)

1. (SLOW MOTION/FREEZE TAG)    PLAY BALL

4. (OBSERVATION GAME)       3. (PLAYGROUND)

   Notes:
```

Lively session! Players liked Observation Game. Next time try Sending Sight Out and Single File.

Keeping track of student skill development can be done with a simple skills chart. A portion of one is shown below.

CHORAL READING
Sequence #3
Workshop #2

Names	Player	Audience	Comments
Tom Davidson	✓		Inventive!
Laura Sanchez	Conductor		First leadership role
Clarence Williams		✓	Still holding back

Sample Workshop

Included for the teacher who is unfamiliar with theater games is a sample workshop sequence. (Seven more workshop sequences will be found in Appendix 1.) These are intended merely as samples. The teacher is encouraged to experiment and test his or her own combinations.

☐ *All the introductory games should be easy, fun, relaxing. Remember, you are a fellow player.*

SEQUENCE #1

	Traditional Games (Warm-ups and wrap-ups)	**Theater Games**
Workshop #1	SINGLE FILE* THREE CHANGES* HERE WE GO ROUND THE MULBERRY BUSH*	MIRROR WHO IS THE MIRROR?
Workshop #2	IDENTIFYING OBJECTS* HERE WE GO ROUND THE MULBERRY BUSH*	PLAY BALL PLAYGROUND
Workshop #3	WHO STARTED THE MOTION?* SINGLE FILE* ADAM'S SONS*	MIRROR SPACE SUBSTANCE
Workshop #4	KITTY WANTS A CORNER* GIVE & TAKE WARM-UP*	SPACE SHAPING (SOLO) TUG OF WAR JUMP ROPE
Workshop #5	A WALK IN THE MOONLIGHT* GIVE & TAKE WARM-UP*	MIRROR FOLLOW THE FOLLOWER INVOLVEMENT IN TWOS
Workshop #6	GIVE & TAKE WARM-UP* NEW YORK (LEMONADE)*	PART OF A WHOLE, ACTIVITY PART OF A WHOLE, OCCUPATION

	Traditional Games (Warm-ups and wrap-ups)	**Theater Games**
Workshop #7		
	MIRROR WHO STARTED THE MOTION?*	MIRROR SOUND
Workshop #8		
	KNOCKING* SINGLE FILE*	LISTENING TO THE ENVIRONMENT PART OF A WHOLE, OCCUPATION
Workshop #9		
	A WALK IN THE MOONLIGHT*	TOUCH & BE TOUCHED HOW OLD AM I? PART OF A WHOLE, RELATIONSHIP
Workshop #10		
	(Read the tale of Sleeping Beauty to the group.) PRINCESS THORN ROSA* (Repeat after playing theater games.)	RELATING AN INCIDENT ADDING COLOR PART OF A WHOLE, ACTIVITY (Use scenes from the story for the *Where*, *Who*, and *What*.)

Playing Area

The playing area is any space in the classroom that can be opened up. It should be large enough to accommodate the playing of the specific game chosen and to allow the audience players to see. The playing area will, of course, change according to the needs of the game. Some games can be played by students from their desks.

Teams

Most theater-game descriptions call for a specific number of players per team. To nurture the spirit of being part of a whole in the classroom, teams should be chosen by random selection. This prevents the pain, self-doubt, and loneliness that almost always arise in players waiting to be picked by the teacher or a team captain.

Counting Off

If a game calls for teams of five players and you have thirty players, you will have, of course, six teams. Before even introducing the game that is to be played, have students count off into sixes — the number of teams you need. Players count off in sixes by calling out (down the row or around the desks) a number in sequence from one to six. They repeat the sequence until all have called a number. Players with the number 1 are on the first team, 2 on the second team, etc. If you have thirty-one players, one team will have an extra player.

If there is a good deal of uneven development within a group, you may need to match players to teams. This can be done by rearranging after the counting-off, but do so without making it obvious to players. Until all the players are able to take the initiative in workshops, place students who are natural catalysts in positions where they can help spark activity. Watch that they do not take over, however. In time, each and every player will develop leadership ability.

Fear of Participation

A student exercising the right to play or not to play may actually be afraid of participation. The fear of disapproval, and the uncertainty of how to win approval, may paralyze the player.

□ Even on a simple "to play or not to play" level, freedom of choice is respected in workshops.

Random counting off for teams almost always throws players into the pool before they can resist. A student who will not play, however, should be kept within view of the playing so that the fear can be eased and eventual participation encouraged. If a player withdraws from the playing during a game, try sidecoaching, **Help your fellow player who isn't playing!** Never call out any player by name, however. The uncertainty as to just which player is not playing brings about group alertness.

Group Agreement

Group agreement is not conformity to the "tyranny of the majority," nor does it come from blindly following a leader. In group agreement, players are given freedom of choice which allows for alternatives. No one is ridiculed for making a suggestion. No one takes over the decision making. Mutual respect arises among players. Everyone has the right to participate to the extent of his or her capacity. Everyone is given and freely takes responsibility for his or her part of the whole. All individuals work at top levels together for the full event.

□ As players begin to trust the games and the approach they will accept differences among themselves.

A community of players is essential to full play. You may elect to work through this handbook from beginning to end, or you may follow one of the workshop sequences. In either case, much of the energy of the early workshops will be spent in building this group of fellow players. Once teams are established and rules of the game presented, teammates are often called upon to agree on the organization and position of all the players within the team. They may have to agree on *Where, Who,* and *What* for a scene or on one sentence for one of the Building a Story games.

□ Fair play, like discipline, arrives when players understand group agreement and are freed from the need to be "best."

At first teams may very well not work in true group agreement as described above. The chance to develop the capacity for independent judgment is offered here. Evaluation periods and playing itself will foster this cooperation. While all players are not equal in skills, all are given equal

□ You as group leader can move from team to team after game presentation, helping headstrong, independent players to cooperate and encouraging fearful, passive children to join in the activities of the group.

opportunity to develop personal responses.

Intensity of involvement should be the gauge of children's capacities and potential. Children with the lowest grades in school may be the most creative in workshops. Their energies unfortunately are not tapped in the regular curriculum. The benefits of playing theater games extend far beyond the teaching of performance skills to children.

Student Sidecoaches

Sidecoach training for students helps build leaders in the classroom. GIBBERISH/ENGLISH, STREETS & ALLEYS, and MIRROR SOUND are all well suited to sidecoach training. For example, when your group has played and understood GIBBERISH/ENGLISH, start a sidecoach training workshop:

"Today we are going to have sidecoach training with GIBBERISH/ENGLISH. We're all going to play at the same time. Everybody count off (for teams of three). Two members of each team will be the players and one the sidecoach. Number 1 will be the first sidecoach. When I call 'Number 2,' then number 2 becomes the sidecoach and numbers 1 and 3 are the players, and so on."

Walk around from unit to unit to help assist sidecoaches. Some student sidecoaches may change from gibberish to English too quickly, others too slowly. Allow each member of the class an opportunity to be a sidecoach.

☐ *As sidecoach, in the position of guiding the needs of others, the most withdrawn student can often blossom magically.*

Designing Workshops to Meet Specific Needs

There are at least three levels of playing: participation (fun and games), problem solving (development of physical and mental perceiving tools), and catalytic action (touching personal intuition). Try to find a balance among these three areas as you adapt these games for your workshops or other schoolroom needs.

☐ *Uneven development of skills is to be expected in workshops. But, when you attend to differences in individual response through sidecoaching, a player will keep up with the others in his or her own way.*

Participation

Theater games are suited to all ages and backgrounds. When necessary, a game should be modified or altered to meet limitations of time, place, physical handicaps, health disorders, fears, etc. There is no program for adaptation. Try to stay close to the presentation in the book at first and make alterations as the need for them arises out of the playing.

Problem Solving

Each game requires the resolution of at least one problem (stated in the focus). The resolution of game problems prepares players for the resolution of many kinds of problems in many other areas of study. If a problem seems to overtax your players, stop the game and do one or more related warm-up exercises.

Catalytic Action

Theater games contain opportunities for tapping the intuitive, the spontaneous, in players. However, breakthrough, like creativity, cannot be programmed. No game will bring optimum results or experience to every player. If some players are not being touched by their workshop experiences, notice what *does* engage them, search for games that will involve them.

Use of Supplementary Materials

For the teacher who wishes to follow a specific theme in workshops or to add games to subjects in the curriculum, the scope and sequence chart (Appendix 2) will be useful. Also consult Index B in Appendix 4, which cross-references games and curriculum areas. However, if curriculum needs or specific themes detract from the *playing*, you are on the wrong track.

A four-part bibliography (Appendix 3) will help you find supplementary teacher-resource material as well as stories and poetry which students can adapt and present in performance. Appendix 1 provides a number of plans for organizing sequences of workshops. Finally, there is a glossary of theater and theater-games terms in Appendix 5.

□ *"Play experience can prepare the student for purposefulness in non-play activities, for true play creates the incentive to use one's best ability."*
— *Neva Boyd*

□ *Excitement and enthusiasm are a precondition to breakthrough.*

□ *Workshop playing allows students to create their own experiences and become masters of their own fate.*

Workshop Checklist (A Review)

Above all, make yourself comfortable during workshops. Choose games you will enjoy. Over time, you and your children will become familiar with the approach, format, and philosophy of theater games and many more choices will open for you all. From time to time, review the following checklist as you prepare your day's order.

1. Leader Preparation
Before presenting any workshop, read through the games you have selected to be sure you understand what is to happen.

2. Counting Off
When teams are called for, *playing begins as soon as players begin to count off.* Players with the same number come together, meet, and form their respective teams. Then, present the game.

3. Lead-ins
Lead-ins are theater games played earlier in workshop sequence that have prepared the group more fully for the game at hand. Depending on the group's readiness and development, you may either repeat the lead-in game in the workshop or simply refer to it as you present the new game. Don't omit a lead-in for fear of not getting through all the games in this handbook. This book includes many times the number of games that any one class could finish in a school year.

☐ *Prepare yourself with many more games than your time will allow in any one workshop. Choose games you feel best suit the needs and talents of your particular class.*

4. Presenting the Games
The focus and description can usually be read aloud to players directly from the book. Try to be enthusiastic but precise. Bring your group into the spirit of play by being playful.

☐ *Begin to play the game yourself at the moment of presenting it.*

5. Lessons
Presenting the games as lessons will reduce excitement and dissipate the energy needed for playing. This approach may build resistance and lead to withdrawal. Since you are offering theater to your class, keep it special and magical — something different from the regular school day.

☐ *Theater-game workshops should be a pleasurable break for you, too.*

6. Examples and Comparisons
Avoid giving examples or making comparisons. Those given in notes to games in this book are for your understanding of the game as the sidecoach. Players usually do

not require these examples. Some players automatically limit their own freedom of choice to fit what has been done before.

7. Resistance

Even if some players do not understand the approach, though some seem to be confused, start to play the game. The playing of the game, sidecoaching during play, and evaluation periods after each turn will remove confusion.

8. Competition

In time, the eagerness to be the first team up will change. Teams will want to be last so as to benefit from the previous teams' evaluation periods.

□ *When a game calls for a single player and all want to go first, have the player most insistent on being first choose the first player.*

9. Audience Players

As each team takes its turn and begins, the remaining teams, while waiting their turns, become involved in the playing as audience. Audience players do not fill in for onstage players, but, from another point of view, are open to what is going on in the playing area and are thus strengthening their perceiving/sensing equipment. As they learn to accept the work of others they will become freer about their own experiments.

□ *Audience players must be in a "state of playing," free of attitudes, analysis, and judgment.*

10. Calling "Curtain!"

When players are ready to begin a game for audience viewing, they are to call "Curtain!" For team play, do not appoint any one player for this task; rather let the players call curtain as a group. You will find many subtle ways of building player responsibility in this handbook. How players' groups call for their curtain can be your barometer to the players' developing sense of the theater.

11. Simultaneous Play

If time is a limiting factor, many games can be played by many teams simultaneously. However, audience players should be used whenever possible for their significant value in the learning process for all.

12. Repeating Games

Do not hesitate to repeat any game that your group enjoys. It is important to repeat key games (MIRROR, GIBBERISH INTRODUCTION, etc.) frequently throughout the year, both as reinforcements of important points and as a gauge of players' development in this work.

13. Trouble-shooting

If a game isn't working, if you and the players are beginning to get fatigued, ask yourself the following questions:

Am I giving enough energy? Am I allowing enough time for the workshop session to avoid rushing? Are sessions too drawn out, too late in the day? Do we need a warm-up game to get us back together? If you think of yourself as a host or hostess to the group, it may help you find the answer more quickly.

14. Wrap-up

Most traditional games and warm-ups will help players as a group quiet down to prepare for the rest of the school day ahead.

□ *If you have selected a game that is beyond you all, stop that game and play another. Do not be afraid to change or alter the rules of the game if such a change clarifies presentation and/or heightens interest, involvement, and response.*

Chapter 2:
WARM-UPS

Singers, athletes, and gymnasts recognize that warming up (whether by practicing scales, swinging a bat, or jogging in place) is essential to performance. Regular warm-ups are always recommended before workshop sessions. Warm-ups warm up! They get blood circulating. Warm-ups are also useful at the end of a low-energy session to lift spirits and invigorate players. On a more practical level, traditional games (OBJECT RELAY, for example) are also valuable in cleaning up scenes requiring sharp timing.

The warm-ups included in this chapter are traditional games, most of them meant to be played out of doors. Other warm-ups (indicated by a ★ following the title) are printed in following chapters. These games, some of them requiring singing, are played by the whole group simultaneously. Each workshop should begin with a few minutes devoted to games of this sort.

☐ *Warm-ups remove the outside distractions players may have brought with them.*

☐ *Singing games have a strong appeal for children because they involve physical movement, cheerful music, and a bit of "play-acting."*

Traditional Games as Warm-Ups

Traditional games are used throughout this work to bring players together, making them willing to accept the rules of each successive game played, eager to reap the benefits of playing. Because they are free of competition and do not reward egotism, they put players into present time, when all are mutually engaged in an experience the outcome of which is unknown.

Traditional games release strong physiological responses: alert bodies, bright eyes, and rosy cheeks. Body weariness ends when involvement begins. Playing traditional games (and playing theater games generally) effectively mobilizes the full physical system, exciting the total physiological response necessary to meet a moment of risk. With no time to think of what to do or how to behave, the player simply acts; he or she does what is necessary. This spontaneous action seems to cleanse the system of the debris of old ideas and conditioned responses. (It is interesting to note that these games produce the same results when played by adults as when played by very young children.)

☐ *Traditional games invoke something like the fight/flight response — spontaneous action for survival.*

Most of the traditional games used in this handbook come from the wonderful body of games collected by Neva Boyd. (See Bibliography A.) Their spirit is deeply rooted in our history and folk life. To quote J. Christian Bay in his foreword to Boyd's *Folk Games of Denmark and Sweden*, "Every trait in the daily life, diversion and festive display of the people has grown out of centuries of usage. On the whole [these games] express ideals as old as the earth itself; and the fundamental thought in the life of any people is to keep the faith of the forefathers." These games touch us, in short, where we are most human.

□ *"Schiller taught us long ago that we are fully human when we are at play."*
—Eric Bentley

Playground Games

Object Relay ★

Description: Two teams. Teams line up side by side. The first player on each team has an object in one hand such as a rolled-up newspaper or a stick. The first player from each team must run to a goal agreed upon, touch it, run back, and hand the object to the next player on the team who must in turn run, touch the goal, run back, give the object to the third player on the team, and so forth until all players have finished and a team has won.

—— SWAT TAG ★ ——————————————

Description: The players are seated in a circle. One of them, A, is given a roll of paper, firmly tied together, twenty or more inches long. A starts the game by lightly touching one after another of the seated players with the roll while moving around the circle. Eventually, A strikes one of them, B, more firmly with the roll of paper and then runs and places the roll on a stool in the center of the circle. A then runs for his seat. B quickly seizes the roll and tries to strike A before he reaches seat. If B succeeds, she replaces the roll on the stool and runs for seat while A gets the roll and tries to strike B with it. If A succeeds, he places the roll on the stool and runs for his seat, pursued by B, who picks up the roll and dashes after him. This play goes on until one of the two players gets safely to his or her seat. The one left in the center starts the game again.

Should the roll fall from the stool at any time, the player who placed it there must replace it before he or she may be seated.

Note: SWAT TAG can be played as an introduction to the games before a seated audience.

—— EXPLOSION TAG ★ ——————————————

Purpose: To crack players' protective armor.

Description: Clear an area of all objects. A 20-by-20 foot space is about right for fifteen players. Half the group plays and half becomes audience. A regular game of tag is played within boundaries. Leader calls out "Not it!" Last player to call out becomes "It." Players may not step outside boundaries. When energy levels are high, teacher will add another rule that when tagged, player must take a moment to "explode." There is no set way to "explode."

Notes: 1. This tag is a natural warm-up, and, although you may have restrictions of time or noise levels, even a minute of EXPLOSION TAG is quite useful.

2. Explosion is a spontaneous action at the moment of being tagged.

3. Ideally, of course, this game should be played out of doors.

Stay within boundaries!
Remember the boundaries!
(When energy level is high):
When you are tagged, take time to explode!
While pursuing another player, keep exploding!
Explode in any way you wish!
Explode!

—— Quick Numbers★ ——————————————

Purpose: To help players focus on a problem.

Description: The players form a semicircle and number off consecutively. Number One, at the head of the line, starts the game by calling another player's number. The player whose number is called responds immediately with still another number, and so on. The player who fails to call a number before the previous caller points at him or her, goes to the foot of the semicircle. All the players below that player move up one place, each taking the number of the person who held the place previously. (Toward the end of the line, therefore, each player's number is changing frequently.) Number One starts the game again by calling a number and the game proceeds as before. When Number One makes a mistake he or she goes to the foot of the line and Number Two becomes Number One, with all the other players again moving up one position.

—— STREETS & ALLEYS ★ ————————————

Description: Fourteen or more players. Select a "dog" and a "cat." All other players form ranks by standing in equal lines with their arms extended sideways or shoulder high. The dog then chases the cat. At a signal from the leader, all turn right a quarter-turn and thus block the progress of the cat or the dog. When the signal is **Streets!**, all players face the sidecoach, and when it is **Alleys!**, all face to the right a quarter-turn. Cat or dog may not crash through a blockade of arms. Have players form the Streets position (see diagram) and practice the change between Alleys and Streets a few times before setting the dog after the cat. When the dog tags the cat, allow them to choose their own replacements.

Notes: 1. This is an excellent tag game for a restricted open space.

2. The success of the game depends upon the alertness of the sidecoach in calling changes at the moment the dog is about to catch the cat or the cat feels too safe. The sidecoach becomes involved in the chase itself and in the fate of the cat, which creates a state of suspense. Acting in crisis (to save or not to save) is stimulation to the whole person and increases alertness and learning capacities.

3. This traditional game is especially useful for training students as sidecoaches. At first, choose student coaches who have a natural alertness to environment, since the game must be kept moving to avoid energy loss and boredom. In time, all players should be given the role of sidecoach so as to learn to handle the momentary crisis the game presents to the sidecoach.

4. This is a useful warm-up in production of plays (often fairy-tale plays) in which there is a strong conflict among characters.

Streets!
Alleys!

Streets:

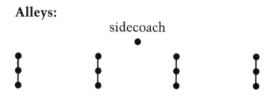

Alleys:

— Streets & Alleys: ——————————
Variations ★

With Slow Motion: Played as in regular game but have dog and cat move in slow motion. Ranks change from Streets to Alleys and back again in slow motion.

With Characters: Give character roles to the runner and chaser: a robber running from a policeman or his victim, a witch or a troll running from a knight, a princess running from an agent of evil.

Without a Sidecoach: Use characters as above. The ranks change from Streets to Alleys, helping or hindering *without* any sidecoaching. This variation brings great excitement in its wake as the group of players (the ranks) nonverbally save the runner or allow the runner to be caught on their own. A room can fill with intense vibrations when the ranks are "thumbs down" on the runner, and when the reverse is true (the runner saved), joy fills the room. This variation should not be used until all players have had experience with the game and are alerted to each other.

— Red Light (Cheese It) ★ ——————————

Description: All the players line up on the starting line, with the one who is "It" fifteen or more feet ahead, on the goal line. All face in the same direction and move forward while "It" counts any number up to ten and adds, "cheese it," e.g., "One, two, three, four, five, cheese it!" Immediately after saying "cheese it," "It" turns around and sends back to the starting line any players whom he or she sees moving even slightly. Counting does not begin again until any offenders are back on the starting line ready to begin. This continues until the last one is over the goal.

Variation: When the first player gets over the goal line he or she becomes "It," and the game starts again.

— DON'T LET GO ★

Description: Players form a circle, holding hands. The teacher, leading a double strand of players, cuts across the circle and intersects the other side. By reversing direction, turning, and turning back on itself in a serpentine fashion, the head of the line crossing other points of the line, the group will tie itself in a knot, unable to move further. Now the group begins to unwind from the teacher's end, continuing to do so until the players have become untangled.

Notes: 1. The more interweaving and reversing the teacher does, the tighter the knot will become.

2. This is a rare playground game quiet enough to be played indoors.

Don't let go!
Don't let go!

Chapter 3:
RHYTHMIC MOVEMENT GAMES

The warm-up games focus on group interaction. The games following, also useful as warm-ups, give players an opportunity to explore and become increasingly aware of the body in motion. They are also useful lead-ins to the Where games (Chapter 9) because they increase players' awareness of the space around them. Establish boundaries around an open area in your classroom in some way so the group will be naturally contained. Chairs and desks can be moved back against the walls, creating a large open space in the center of the room.

Reading the sidecoaching directly from the book as you move about with your fellow players is the only effective approach to take. Let the sidecoaching work on you too as you walk about the room. This type of exercise will come more easily to teachers who have had some dance and movement experience.

□ *In theater-game workshops, students should feel free to explore.*

—— OCEAN WAVE ★ ———————

Purpose: To help players move in unison.

Description: The players arrange their chairs close together in a circle. One player then goes into the center, which leaves one vacant chair. The center player calls "Shift right (or left)" and changes the call whenever he or she wishes. The players endeavor to keep the chair on the right or left occupied while shifting as directed. In the meantime the center player tries to get a seat. Whoever is at fault in case he or she succeeds exchanges places with the center player.

— A WALK IN THE MOONLIGHT ★ —

Focus: On full participation.

Description: Divide group into teams of two. Couples stand in two lines all facing the head of the line, with inside hands joined and raised high, forming arches, as all begin singing. Last couple walks under the arches to the head of the line and takes its place at the head with hands raised. Other couples follow in turn, each beginning on "My partner and I . . ." Continue until the original head couple marches under and leads off. Or the lines may face in the opposite direction and play the game through again.

Variation: Simply have players sing while walking hand in hand at a leisurely pace around the schoolroom, looking at all that is around them as if for the first time.

Note: This traditional singing game has been played as a warm-up to workshop sessions for adult professional actors, who derived as much pleasure from it as do young children. It appears in *Folk Games and Gymnastic Play*, by Neva L. Boyd and Dagny Pederson (Chicago: H.T. Fitz-Simons Co., Inc.).

My part-ner and I will take a walk, a walk a walk a moon-light walk

—— Slow Motion/Freeze Tag ★ ——

Purpose: To explore physical movement and expression.

Focus: On moving in complete slow motion.

Description: Many players. (If time allows, half the group is audience to the other half's playing.) After a short warm-up of EXPLOSION TAG, a game of freeze tag is played in very slow motion and within restricted boundaries. Appoint the first "It." All players run, breathe, duck, look, etc. in very slow motion. Immediately upon tagging another player, "It" must freeze in the exact tagging position. The new "It" proceeds in slow motion and freezes in position as another player is tagged, who becomes "It." All untagged players must stay within boundaries and move in slow motion between and around frozen players (as around trees in a forest). Game continues until all are frozen.

Notes: 1. The space the game is played in must be restricted or the game can become too time consuming. If the group is overlarge, two taggers are recommended. At the end, coach, ***Taggers tag each other!***

2. In true slow motion there is fluidity of movement.

3. This is a variation on the traditional game KING OF THE MOUNTAIN.

Run in slow motion!
Breathe in slow motion!
Duck away from "It" in very slow motion!
Tag in slow motion!
Lift your feet in slow motion!
Stay within bounds in very slooooooow motion!

Is there a difference between moving slowly and moving in slow motion?
Audience, did you see a difference between moving slowly (start, stop, start, stop) and moving in slow motion?

RHYTHMIC MOVEMENT

Purpose: To discover natural body movement.

Focus: On a rhythmic movement of the body.

Description: Ten to fifteen players, as a team, sit or stand in playing area. Others observe.

Part 1: Sidecoach calls out any object, such as a train, washing machine, spaceship, bicycle, etc. Each player instantly, without reflection, makes some movement that the object suggests. When movements have become rhythmical and easy, players should move around playing area, accompanied by music if available. Sidecoach, ***Forget your object! Feel your rhythm!***

Part 2: The sidecoach then quickly defines a setting (see example below). Without stopping rhythmic movements, players transform their movement into something else, developing characters and actions appropriate to the setting.

Example: A circus with ringmaster, clowns, liontamers (and lions), tightrope walkers, trapeze artists, elephants, horses, onlookers, etc.

Notes: 1. If individual players have difficulty finding characters, the sidecoach may move into the playing area to help. This must be done quickly without stopping the rhythm.

2. GIVE & TAKE WARM-UP is a useful preparation for this game.

3. In hunting societies, dances were and are performed to bring good luck to the hunters. One dancer might play the part of a bear or an elephant or a kangaroo or of a "magical" animal like a crow. The dancers did not do imitations of these animals, but aimed at giving an impression of their "spirit." That sort of impression is what one looks for in this game.

Forget your object!
Let your movement suggest your character!
Feel your rhythm!
Interact with one another!

Part 2:
Transform!
Transform!
Keep your rhythm going!

Audience, did the rhythmic movement develop the character in the given situation?
Did the players give and take?
Players, do you agree?

— NO MOTION —

Purpose: To aid in understanding elements of movement.

Focus: On the "no motion"—the moments of quiet rest—within every movement.

Description: Part 1: Players raise their arms, breaking up the flow of movement into a series of stills or frames as on a filmstrip.

Part 2: When so coached, players raise arms up and down in regular speed but focus on the pauses within the total flow of movement.

Variation: Players (full group if possible) walk around the room or play area focusing on "no motion."

Notes: 1. Properly executed, this exercise gives a physical feeling and understanding of keeping out of the way. By focusing on "no motion," hands, legs, etc., move effortlessly without conscious volition. You are at rest in "no motion"—without attitude about the action.

2. You might say that a running back in professional football is in "no motion" as he runs downfield. His mind is in total rest so he can more clearly see and hear, and thus spontaneously select the route to take to avoid blockers.

3. *No motion!* used as a sidecoaching directive keeps the player quiet. This loss of concern releases fear, anxiety, and the like, and leaves a clear mind.

4. All of the sight, hearing, and touching exercises (Chapter 6) can be added to the walk around the room (see Variation) if time and inclination allow.

Part 1:

Raise your arms as in a series of frames in a filmstrip!
Focus on the feeling of "no motion" as you raise your arms!
Focus on doing nothing!
Bring your arms down in "no motion"!
Let your arms do the work!

Part 2:

Raise your arms in regular speed, focusing on "no motion"!
Triple your speed, focusing on "no motion"!
Up and down! Normal speed in "no motion"!

Variation:

Focus on the periods of "no motion"!
Let your body walk around the room in "no motion"!

How many felt "no motion"?
Were you moving your arms?
Were your arms moving themselves?

Chapter 4:
SPACE WALKS

Rhythmic movement games focus on exploration and awareness of one's body in movement. Space walks extend this exploration, giving students a chance to move through and explore the familiar space of the classroom, giving that space a new immediacy. Space walks should be given often as warm-ups.

Many new teachers may discover that these games require a change in approach. Inhibiting a student's wandering, experimental thought may seem to be necessary to good discipline but may actually shut fast a door in the face of the seeker, dreamer, or adventurer. In theater-game workshops, students can be freed to explore.

If it proves difficult, however, to stay on focus, come back to these games when the classroom atmosphere is more relaxed. After students have played other sensory or observation games such as SENDING SIGHT OUT, they will be better prepared for the space walks.

☐ *Remember, it takes courage to move out into the new, the unknown.*

TOUCH & BE TOUCHED/ SEE & BE SEEN

Purpose: To help create greater sensory awareness in players.

Focus: On touching the object *and allowing the object to touch you.*

Description: Players are allowed to move freely around the stage space. They are coached to touch a succession of objects and, when the object is felt, to allow the object to touch them.

Notes: 1. Remember to keep players moving and to allow time between sidecoaching directives.

2. Teachers should join in this exercise with players while sidecoaching.

3. Allow players to touch and be touched, see and be seen. It is difficult for many to allow themselves to be seen.

4. The sidecoaching phrase **Take a ride on your own body!** helps players experience detachment, thus finding greater involvement. In some twentieth-century theater, this sense of detachment is central to good acting. Bertolt Brecht called it "the alienation effect."

Allow the space to move through you and you move through the space!
Take a ride on your own body and look at the scenery around you!
Touch an object in the space— a tree, a cup, a piece of clothing, a chair!
When you touch the object, feel it, allow it to touch (feel) you!
(Vary objects.)
Touch a fellow player and allow your fellow player to touch you!
Touch and be touched!
(Vary players.)
See an object!
The moment you really see it, allow the object to see you!
(Vary objects.)
See a fellow player! Allow the fellow player to see you!

Was it difficult to allow yourself to be touched . . . to be seen?
How did you feel about touching and being touched?
Could you explain the difference to an audience?
What would you say?

FEELING SELF WITH SELF ★ ————————————

Purpose: To discover full-body perception of self.

Focus: On feeling self with the body part that is sidecoached.

Description: Players sit quietly and respond.

Notes: 1. FEELING SELF WITH SELF is one of the basic warm-up exercises.

2. Coach *Keep your eyes open!* if necessary. Closed eyes can be a withdrawal.

3. This is a good exercise for relaxing and refreshing students.

Feel your feet in your socks!
Feel your socks on your feet!
Feel your feet in your shoes!
Feel your socks on your legs!
Feel your legs in your socks!
Feel your pants or skirt over your legs!
Feel your legs in your pants!
Feel your blouse or shirt against your back and your back underneath your blouse or shirt!
Feel your ring on your finger!
Feel your finger in your ring!
Feel the hair on your head and your eyebrows on your forehead!
Feel your tongue in your mouth!
Feel your ears!
Try to feel the inside of your head!
Feel all the space around you!
Now let the space feel you!

Was there any difference between feeling your ring on your finger and feeling your finger in the ring?

—— SPACE WALK #1 ——

Purpose: To familiarize players with the element (space) they live in.

Focus: On feeling space with the whole body.

Description: Players walk around and physically investigate space as an unknown substance.

Notes: 1. As in all space walks, the teacher walks with the group while coaching the exercise. Use your players' physical characteristics (tight mouth, hunched shoulders, etc.) as your guide to coaching space walks. For example, if one player has a fixed eye expression, you might say, **Put space where your eyes are! Let your sight pass through your eyes!** If you single out one player's area of tension, do not let that player realize it. What helps one helps all.

2. A simple introduction to space substance is to ask players what is between you and them. Players will respond with "air," "atmosphere," "space." Whatever the players call it, ask that they consider whatever is between, around, over, or under them as "space substance" for the purpose of these exercises.

3. Give some time between each coaching phrase for players to have the experience.

4. You may wish to delay trying these games until you are more comfortable with this approach to space.

5. Do not belabor evaluation of space walks.

6. See also FEELING SELF WITH SELF.

Walk around and feel the space around you!
Investigate it!
Feel the space against your back!
Your neck!
Feel the space with your body and let your hands be as one with your body!
Feel space inside your mouth!
Along the outside of your body!
Feel your body shape as you move through space!
Now let the space feel you! Your face! Your arms! Your whole body!
Keep your eyes open!
Wait! Don't force it!
You go through the space and let the space go through you!

Did anyone get a feeling of space or of letting space feel you?

— SPACE WALK #2 —

Purpose: To feel surrounding space.

Focus: On holding yourself together or letting space support you, as sidecoached.

Description: Players walk around the room and hold themselves together to allow the space to support, as sidecoached.

Notes: 1. As in SPACE WALK #1, teacher walks with the group while coaching the exercise. Allow time between coaching phrases for the experience.

2. Letting space support you does not mean losing control or going limp. Player is to allow the body its proper alignment.

3. Play this a few times. Everyone finds pleasure in it. Wait until players know one another.

4. Change back and forth between sole support and space support, until players experience the difference.

5. Students will have a tendency to move in slow motion as though they were underwater. Ask them, "What slows down the movements of divers?"

You go through the space and let space go through you!
As you walk along, go inside your body and feel tenseness!
Feel your shoulders!
Up and down the spine!
Feel your inside from the inside!
Observe! Take note!
You are your only support!
You are holding your face together! Your toes on your feet!
Your whole skeleton together!
You are holding your body together!
If you did not hang on to yourself, you would fall into a thousand pieces!
Now change!
Walk through the space and let the space support you!
Your body will understand!
Note your body feeling!
Put space where your eyes are!
Allow the space to support your face! Your shoulders!
Now change!
You are again your only support!

Was there a difference between you as your only support and allowing space to support you?

—— SPACE WALK #3: SKELETON ——————————

Purpose: To physically feel the body.

Focus: On physical movement of one's skeleton in space.

Description: Players walk through space focusing on the skeletal movement of bones and joints.

Note: Sidecoach players back to their own body form.

Part 1:

You go through the space and let the space go through you!
Feel your skeleton moving in space! But avoid seeing a picture of your skeleton!
Feel the movement of every joint!
Allow your joints to move freely!
Feel the movement of your spine!
Let your head rest on its own pedestal!
Feel your skull with your skull!
Now put space where your cheeks are! Around your arm bones! Between each disk in your spinal column! Put space where your stomach is!
Feel your own form once more! The outer outline of your whole body in space!
Feel where the space ends and you begin!

Part 2:

Now pick up the body and facial expression of another person! From the inside! The lips! The eyes! The skeleton! Get the full physical expression of that person! Now, take on the feelings (emotions) of that person! Keep the physical expression!

Did you feel your own skeleton moving in space?

SPACE WALK BLINDFOLDED

Purpose: To develop full-body sensory awareness.

Focus: On moving about the playing area, while blind-folded, as if one could see.

Description: Two or more players define a simple scene and set up the playing area with real hand props, set pieces, chairs, and tables. Playing area should be flat, with all sharp, pointed objects removed. Real prop blindfolds are needed. The *What* (activity) is to be one that requires handling and passing many objects, such as a tea party.

Variation: This game can also be played without props by having teams move through the playing area, each player respecting the other's space.

Notes: 1. In the beginning, loss of sight produces anxiety in some players, who stay immobilized in one spot. Sidecoaching and use of a prop telephone will help. Ring the bell (vocally if necessary) to call the player (by name) to the phone. It is not necessary to converse. Player will carry on.

2. Contact through handing around real props is necessary to the success of this exercise.

3. Ask students which of the senses they rely on most. Which is second most important? If one of the senses is taken away do the others make up the difference?

Follow through on that move!
Find the chair you were looking for!
Be adventurous!
Hang up your hat!

Variation:
Walk in and around your fellow players!
Keep to your own space!
Respect the space of fellow players!

Did players move naturally?
Were all movements integrated into the scene?
Was this integration interesting?
(If a player is looking for a chair, he or she might swing an arm or lurch as if such moves were part of the character.)

Chapter 5:
TRANSFORMATION GAMES
Making the Invisible Visible

Workshop space-object games provide an ideal orientation for players and offer countless opportunities for allowing inner feeling and thoughts to break through. Objects used in these games are made of space — the very stuff that surrounds us all. A "space ball" is not an imaginary ball. It is a part of space — thin air — that is called "ball." If a student tosses an imaginary ball, he or she may be conscious of a real ball that is missing, that is not *there*. The player is working with the *idea* of a ball. A space ball, on the other hand, is a ball that is coming into existence. In practice this distinction is not abstract. Any audience can see the difference.

The use of space objects in a theater setting is often thought of as pantomime. In fact, the use of space objects is different from true pantomime, a venerable art form — sister to the dance, cousin of sleight-of-hand. The player who creates a space object is not attempting to create an artful illusion for an audience. Rather, he or she experiences the awakening of an intuitive area which can perceive the space object as it emerges. When the invisible becomes visible, we have theater magic!

In effect, an invisible ball thrown to a fellow player in PLAY BALL helps the player to share, to make a connection with the fellow player who also accepts and catches the invisible ball. To help them achieve this connection, sidecoach **Keep the ball in space and not in your head!** and **Give the ball its time in space!** In a short time, all in the room will intuitively perceive the unseen space substance as real! Space — the invisible — becomes visible through the collaboration of players throwing and catching the space object.

□ *Space objects should be looked upon as thrusts of the invisible inner self into the visible world. Students who create space objects will discover that reaching out is reaching in.*

□ *Use of the intuition cannot be taught. One must be tripped into it.*

□ *Among players, real communication is often invisible.*

Ideas, terms, and phrases important to this chapter:

Breakthrough: The point at which a player's spontaneity arises to meet a crisis; the moment of letting go, of seeing things from a different point of view, reaching out beyond past limitations.

Imagination: A part of the intellect. When we ask someone to imagine something, we are asking him or her to go into a personal frame of reference, which may be limited. When we ask someone to *see*, we are placing that person in an objective situation in which reaching out into the environment can take place, where further awareness is possible.

Playing safe: A defense strategy; a means by which players cheat themselves of an unexpected discovery. Playing safe keeps players from tapping and using new energy.

Transformations: New creations, visible events, which arise out of heightened physical movement, from the exchange of moving energy among players.

Explore and heighten!: Be on the lookout for small nuances and details which should not pass unnoticed. Coaching *Explore and heighten!* increases the energy level, brings a broader, intensified experience, and discourages pre-planning.

Out of the head! Into the space!: When coached during playing, these phrases produce an actual field — space — upon which the energy exchange, the playing, takes place among players. *Out of the head, into the space!* is recommended both for sidecoaching and for evaluation periods. The youngest player personally responds to and clearly senses this new invisible area — space — as real! *Out of the head and into the space!* does away with or prevents conditioned responses. Full-body perception is strengthened and energy exchange is increased.

Take a ride on your own body!: This creates great detachment during games.

SPACE SUBSTANCE

Purpose: To "sense" space.

Focus: On the space substance between palms of players' hands.

Description: Part 1: Divide group into two teams — players and audience. Using the first team, each player working individually, have them move hands up/down, close together/far apart, and every which way just so long as palms are always facing. Players are to focus on the space substance between palms.

    Part 2: With teams of two, players stand opposite each other, three or four feet apart, with the cupped palms of their hands facing the palms of fellow player. Players are to move hands up/down, closer together/farther apart, and keep focus on the space substance between the four palms of their hands.

Notes: 1. This exercise quickly gives players an experience of space substance. However, in time players must let partial focus on palms of hands dissolve in order to feel head-to-toe freedom to handle, play with, and respond to this most unique "stuff."

    2. Audience team players will benefit from watching this game. However, if time is short, the full group may play this exercise simultaneously.

    3. Students studying chemistry will be aware that air is a "substance" (oxygen mixed with other gases) which does not exist in outer space or on worlds like the moon, which has no atmosphere.

Part 1:

Move hands back and forth!
Anywhere!
But keep palms always facing!
Focus on the space material
between your palms!
Let palms go where they will!
Feel the space material
between!
Move the space material about
between your palms!
Play with it! Let it thicken!

Part 2:

Turn and face a partner!
Two palms facing two palms of
partner!
Feel the space material between
the four palms!
Play with the space material!
Move it about!
Use your whole bodies!
Focus on the space between your
palms and let it thicken if it
does!

Audience, did players let focus
on space substance work for them?
Did the players imagine
the space material or did they
really feel it?
Players, do you agree?
Did space material begin to
thicken for you?

— Space Shaping (Solo) —

Purpose: To discover how "space" can be manipulated.

Focus: On allowing space substance to take shape as an object.

Description: Each player works individually. Player focuses on and plays with space substance, moving it about with hands, arms, and the whole body. Without forcing anything, player allows the space substance to take shape as an object, if it does.

Notes: 1. Players are not to stand rigidly moving hands aimlessly in the air. An object can only take shape when players are involved with the space substance from head to toe and moving/flowing with full physical energy on the problem.

2. Help players distinguish between allowing an object to take shape and imposing form on the space substance. This exercise does not call for invention.

3. See Space Substance, Note #3. If it becomes very cold, oxygen *does* thicken into a liquid.

Play with the space substance!
Move it about with your whole body! Heighten it!
Full body!
Explore and heighten!
If an object begins to take shape, let it grow!
Feel its weight! Its texture!
Keep it in space!
Out of the imagination!
Focus on the space object!
Feel the object!
(Coach for specific object's characteristics/qualities if object begins to appear.)

Did you force an object or let an object take shape?
Was the object in space or in your imaginations?

SPACE SHAPING FOR TEAMS

Purpose: To explore a new kind of nonverbal communication.

Focus: On allowing space substance to take shape as an object.

Description: Part 1: Teams of two (many teams may play simultaneously). Players both focus on and play with the space substance between them, moving space substance about with full-body/head-to-toe involvement, remaining open for a space object to appear, if it does.

Part 2: Teams of three, four, five, or more. Players form a circle and focus on the space substance within the ring of their bodies. Playing with head-to-toe involvement with the space substance, players remain open for a space object to appear and take shape.

Notes: 1. The space object will not take shape between players if one player manipulates the others into accepting "his" object.

2. Audience players are of benefit to this series of exercises. However, if time is limited, the full group can play at once. Start with SPACE SHAPING (SOLO), all players working individually. For Part 1 (above), have players turn and take a partner and continue. For Part 2, simply take two or three teams of two and gather them into a circle and continue the sidecoaching.

3. In the beginning, not all players will be successful. Allow for this without discussion. If one or more of the audience players insist that some players did not solve the problem, simply note that not all problems are solved the first time. The important thing is this: were the players working to solve the problem?

Let space thicken!
Let it happen!
Explore and heighten!
Stay with the object!
Keep the object between you!
Don't rush it!
Follow the follower![1]
Keep the object between you!
In space!
(Sidecoach for texture, weight, other object qualities only if an object begins to take shape from space substance.)

Audience players, did you begin to recognize an object?
Was the object in space or in players' imaginations?
Players, do you agree?

[1]See Chapter 8.

— TUG OF WAR —————————————

Purpose: To awaken the invisible communication among players.

Focus: On keeping the space rope as a connecting link between players.

Description: Pair off in twos. One at a time, each player tries to pull the other over a center line, exactly as in playground tug of war. Here, however, the rope is not visible but made of space substance. Ask players to **Pick a partner of equal strength!** This message is received with laughter. It creates mutuality — a bond — contest not competition. As each team plays, the others observe.

Notes: 1. Read chapter heading and notes on SPACE SUBSTANCE, above.

2. Play the space rope and space ball games with your group until the phenomenon of objects in space, not in the head, has been experienced by everyone and is understood by your group.

3. As your group becomes facile with this game played in pairs, add more and more players to both ends of the rope.

4. Invisible communication and agreement may explain some extraordinary events. Most scientists believe that flying saucers, abominable snowmen, etc. are sighted when many people "see" something that isn't really there.

Keep the rope between you!
Use your full bodies to pull! Your back! Your feet!
Stay on the same rope!
Pull! Pull! Pull!

Audience, were the players on the same rope? Did the rope connect players? Was the rope in space or in the players' heads? Players, was the rope in space or in your heads? Do players agree with audience? Does audience agree with players?

— JUMP ROPE —————————————

Purpose: On interaction among members of a large group, using space substance.

Focus: On keeping a rope moving in space.

Description: Count off into teams of four or more, or allow random groupings. Each team will play its own game of jump rope, with some players turning the rope while the other players jump. Play until everyone has had a chance to *turn* the rope. (Turning the rope requires more concentration than jumping.)

Notes: 1. As in the regular jump rope game, the jumper who misses must exchange places with a player turning the rope.

2. Jump rope variations: Double Dutch, High and Higher, Lindy Loop, etc.

Stay on the same rope!
Use your whole body to play the game!

Did players keep the rope in space, or in their heads?

—— Play Ball ——————————————————————

Purpose: To focus players' attention on a moving space object.

Focus: On keeping the ball in space and out of the head.

Description: Players count off into two large teams. First, one team is the audience, then the other. Working individually within the team, players each start to toss a ball against a wall, etc. The balls are all made of space substance. When the players are all in motion, sidecoach to change the speed at which balls are moving.

Notes: 1. Read chapter heading and notes on Space Substance, above.

2. Words used by the teacher in the presentation of this game must be carefully chosen. Players are not asked to pretend or imagine. Players are simply sidecoached to keep the ball in space and out of the head.

3. The player knows when the ball is in the space or in the head. When it is in the space it will "appear" to player and audience alike.

4. The evaluation questions are important in that they acknowledge the audience's responsibility to observe the emergence if it should occur. The audience is as responsible for keeping focus as is the playing team.

5. After evaluation of the first team, have the next team play. Did the second team benefit from evaluation of the first team?

6. Emphasize use of full body to keep the ball in motion. Players should leave the game with all the physical aftereffects of having played an active game of catch.

Variations: 1. Play same game with a space-substance ball that changes weight. As ball becomes lighter and heavier, players' bodies may seem to become lighter and heavier or to move in slow motion. Do not bring this point to players' attention during play.

2. Play other games — dodge ball, volleyball, baseball — with space-substance balls.

3. Note that different planets have different gravity. Baseballs on the moon would be much lighter than on earth. Ask students what a game of baseball on the moon might be like.

*Use your **full body** to throw the ball!*
Keep your eye on the ball!
Change! Speed it up!
Throw and catch the ball as fast as you can!
Back and forth as fast as you can!
Normal once more!
Allow the ball its time in space!
The ball is moving in verrry slooooooow motion!
Catch the ball in very slow motion!
Now the ball is moving normally!

Variation #1:
The ball is becoming lighter!
It is one hundred times lighter!
Now it is becoming heavy!
Use your whole body to throw the ball!
Keep your eyes on the ball!

Players, did you imagine the ball or did you actually feel it?
Audience, do you agree with players?
Was the ball pretended or was there a ball made of space?
Players, did you allow the ball its time in space?
Audience, do you agree?

— PLAYGROUND

Purpose: To discover a variety of ways of using space substance in games.

Focus: On keeping play objects moving in and taking up space.

Description: Full group divides into teams of differing sizes, and each team chooses a playground game requiring equipment or play objects. (These might include not only ball games such as baseball, basketball, or volleyball but games using toys, like jacks, marbles, and tiddlywinks.) All rules of the chosen game must be followed. Players must keep the ball or equipment in the space and out of their heads. Teams scattered around the room play different games simultaneously as on a playground. All games are to be played with space-substance objects.

Notes: 1. PLAYGROUND is ideal for recess or physical education periods on the playground.

2. If players are beginning to grasp the idea of playing with space-substance objects, the whole playing area should be full of excitement, energy, and fun. PLAYGROUND should be used often. The author has seen as many as five innings of baseball played with space objects.

3. This and other playground games will benefit from audience evaluations. Audience teams can sidecoach, ***Keep your eye on the ball!***

(Move from group to group and join in if your presence will add to the playing.)

Don't lose track of your object!
Use your full body to throw the ball!
Heighten that movement!
More energy!
Heighten!

Audience, was this playing object only an idea?
Was it in the space or imaginary?
Players, do you agree?

—— DODGE BALL ——————————————

Purpose: To work with a rapidly moving space object.

Focus: On keeping the ball in space, seeing it as others see it.

Description: Count off into large groups (ten players or more). Players standing in a circle try to hit a center player with a space ball. If the center player is hit, he or she changes places with the player who threw the ball. It is a foul if a player is hit above the waist (see Note #2 below).

Notes: 1. Remember, if players do not leave this game with all the same indications (excitement, physical warmth, pink cheeks, out-of-breath state) they have after playing with a real ball, then the players were pretending.

2. The rule of "no hitting above the waist" is an amusing one for the players inasmuch as there is no material ball. The rule is followed, however.

3. Space-object games are good exercise. Ask students what makes them breathe more heavily after a game; why do their bodies require more oxygen.

Play with your whole bodies!
Keep your eye on the ball!
Keep the ball in space!
No hitting above the waist!
Throw and catch with your full bodies!
(If center is hit):
Change places with the player who threw the ball!

Players, was the ball in space, or in your imaginations?
Audience, was the ball in space or were the players pretending?
Players, do you agree?
Were all players using the same ball?

—— INVOLVEMENT IN TWOS——————————

Purpose: Making the invisible visible, using space objects as theatrical props.

Focus: On the object between players.

Description: Teams of two players agree on an object and begin an activity determined by the object itself, such as folding bedsheets or pulling taffy.

Notes: 1. It is natural for players to want to plan the action out in advance, which defeats spontaneity and results in awkwardness. To avoid playwriting, have each team write on a slip of paper the name of an object. Place all the slips in a container. Each team takes a slip just before its turn.

2. Players are not to build a story around the object, and therefore there should be little need for dialogue. Suggest that the object be one which is ordinarily handled.

3. This is a dramatic situation without conflict. While most playwrights assume that conflict is central to a scene, good actors in performance generally try to help one another.

Keep the object between you!
Keep the object in the space!
Make the object real!
Show!
Don't tell!
Use your whole body!

What was the object?
Did players show or tell?
Did players work together?
Did this team benefit from preceding team's evaluation?
Players, do you agree?

— INVOLVEMENT WITH THREE OR MORE ——

Purpose: To encourage team agreement and joint participation.

Focus: On keeping an object in space between players.

Description: Teams of three or more players. They agree on an object which cannot be used without involving all of them. Players participate in a joint action in which all move the same object. For example: pulling a fishnet, portaging a canoe, pushing a stalled car.

Note: INVOLVEMENT IN TWOS will, like TUG OF WAR, almost automatically keep players involved with each other through the object. This game may tend to confuse players, i.e., one player may direct the other two in moving the object rather than all three becoming directly involved.

Work together!
You need each other to solve the problem!
Keep the object in the space!
Keep the object between you!

Did players work together?
Or was one of them not needed for the task?
Players, did you need each other to move the object?
Audience, do you agree?
Did this team benefit from the preceding team's evaluation?

— FINDING OBJECTS IN THE ——————
IMMEDIATE ENVIRONMENT

Purpose: To make the invisible visible.

Focus: On receiving objects from the environment.

Description: Three or more players agree on a simple relationship and a discussion which involves everyone, such as a PTA meeting or family conference. Discussion might take place around a space table. During the course of the meeting, each player finds and handles as many space objects as possible. Players do not plan ahead what these objects will be.

Notes: 1. This is a two-way problem. The onstage occupation, the meeting, must be continuous, while the preoccupation, the focus, must be worked on at all times. Some players will keep the meeting going and neglect the focus. Sidecoach accordingly!

2. When this problem is solved, much to everyone's excitement, endless objects appear: lint is found on a neighbor's coat, dust floats through the air, and pencils come out from behind ears. All players have the opportunity to discover this for themselves.

Take your time!
Let objects appear!
Keep the discussion going!
Share your voice!
Keep in contact with each other!
The objects are found in the space!
Help your fellow player who isn't playing!

Did objects appear or were they invented?
Did players see each other's objects and use them?
Did players refer to objects or actually contact them?
Players, did you allow objects to appear?

—— It's Heavier When It's Full ——————

Purpose: To discover the properties of theatrical props through use of space objects.

Focus: On keeping the weight of objects in space and out of the head.

Description: Count off into teams of ten players. Teams agree on an activity in which containers must be filled, emptied, and filled again. Two or three members of a team can carry objects together. Some examples are picking apples, filling a treasure chest, carrying water.

Notes: 1. Given an opportunity, children will discover an important theatrical truth with this game: receptacles on stage are almost never so heavy as they would be if they were real. (See *Improvisation for the Theater,* pp. 291-2.)

2. Also have players handle objects of different weights. They might shovel sand, pitch hay, lift weights, etc.

3. Admirers of traditional mime will know that for a mime, an object has only those properties which directly relate to the actor. We never know the color, material, or size of Marceau's suitcase. We know only that it is too heavy to carry.

Feel the weight in your legs!
Your back!
Not only your arms!
Feel weight with your whole body!

Did players show the difference in weight (bodily response)?
Players, do you agree
with audience?
Why is it necessary for the player to know that "it's heavier when it's ful

— TRANSFORMATION OF OBJECTS —

Purpose: To make the invisible visible, sensing the true nature of objects.

Focus: On the use of physical full-body movement and energy to create change/transformation in a space object.

Description: Large teams of ten or more players stand in a circle. First player, focusing on the space substance between palms of the hands, moving space substance this way and that with head-to-toe movement, allows an object to take shape and then passes it on to the next player. The second player handles and plays with that object and allows the space substance to take another shape, if it does, and then passes it on to the next player. Players are not to change the object they receive. If the object transforms itself, the transformation will come out of heightened, exaggerated playing with and handling of the object received. If there is no transformation, players simply pass on the object received to next player. For example, if a player is handed a yo-yo, it might transform into a bird or into an accordion, depending on how playing energy is heightened and used. Objects are used and handed on to players all around the circle in turn.

Note: Full-body movement brings up the physical energy necessary for transformation. Coach for full-body response.

Use your whole body to play with the object!
Turn it around!
Don't plan to change it!
Play with the object!
Feel the energy come through your whole body into the object!
Into the space substance!
Let your whole body respond!

Players, did objects transform themselves?
Or did you change the object?
Did any of you get the feeling of the objects transforming themselves?

— DIFFICULTY WITH SMALL OBJECTS —

Purpose: To cope with problems presented by space objects.

Focus: On overcoming difficulty with objects.

Description: Single player becomes involved with a small space object or article of clothing which presents some problem. Some examples include opening a tightly sealed jar, dealing with a caught zipper, a jammed drawer, tight boots.

Notes: 1. When players seem ready, two or more may participate in this exercise at a time.

2. Resistance to the focus shows itself in a player who intellectualizes (playwrites) the problem. Instead of having a physical difficulty with the object, he or she may, for instance, have a hole in his or her shoe and place a dollar bill over the hole, which is a "joke" and a total avoidance of the exercise.

Make the object real!
Share with the audience!
Explore the object!
Heighten the difficulty!

Audience, what was the object?

—— THE OBJECT MOVES THE PLAYERS ——————

Purpose: To give space objects movement, even life.

Focus: On the object moving the players.

Description: Any number of players agree on an object, such as a sailboat, roller coaster, elephant, etc., which is to move all simultaneously.

Variation: Let each player choose an object which is alive or can be set in motion: a cat, insect, yo-yo, kite, etc. The identity and nature of the object are communicated to the audience by the way the player handles it.

Notes: 1. If focus is kept totally on the moving object, players begin to feel the object among them and audience players will recognize it.

2. Players not ready to focus with concentration may watch fellow players to know when to move. Keep coaching **Let the object move you!** over and over as an aid in breaking this dependency.

3. Often players will "let go" and let the object move them only after constant coaching. Each team should play the game until this experience is shared by most.

4. In big special-effects movies, film actors on the set often have to act as though they were being affected by large objects and forces which actually aren't present. The ship that is sinking, for example, is only a small piece of decking, the storm is provided by a man with a garden hose, the raging Pacific is a big tank of luke-warm water.

Feel the object!
Let the object move you!
You're all in it together!
Don't let it disappear!
Let your whole body show
the object's life!
Feel the object move you!
Heighten!
Let the object move you!

Audience, did players allow the object to move them?
Did they initiate movement?
Did players move by watching the other players?
Players, did you make this a Mirror game (reflection of others), or did you keep the focus?

— ADD A PART —————————————————

Purpose: To help players work together in dealing with a large and complicated space object.

Focus: On using part of a whole object in space — out of the head.

Description: Eight to ten players per team. First player uses or makes contact with part of a larger object that only he or she has in mind and then leaves the playing area. One by one, players use or contact other parts of the whole object until the whole object is left in space.

Example: First player sits and uses a steering wheel, second wipes the windshield, third opens the car door, and so on.

Notes: 1. This game is similar to PART OF A WHOLE, OBJECT, but players do not become the part with their bodies; rather they use parts of a larger space object in the playing area.

2. Players are not to build their part of the object with tools, but by *using* that part. The windshield in the above example can be added by wiping its surface. The focus in this game is on the appearance — when the invisible becomes visible.

3. All stage actors know that, up close, sets are rarely what they seem. They may look like real rooms from the point of view of the audience, but looking downstage one can see that the cabinets have no interiors, the brickwork is styrofoam, the props are papier-mâché.

Let us see what you see!
Give the part its place in space!
Stay with the same whole object!
Other players see the whole through the parts left by others!
Avoid planning your part!
Use what was left by others and let your own part appear!

Audience, what was the complete object?
Were the added parts in the space or in the players' heads?
Players, do you agree?
First player, was that the object you had in mind?

Chapter 6:
SENSORY GAMES

After warm-ups the group should be relaxed and receptive — ready for a short discussion of the senses and their value as tools. In stage life, it may be pointed out, mashed potatoes are often served in place of ice cream, and stone walls are actually made of wood, canvas, and styrofoam (indeed, in improvisational theater, props and scenery are often space objects). It is not convincing when actors merely behave as if these substitutes were real. In time, students will begin to appreciate that actors use their sensory equipment, their physical bodies, to make visible for an audience what is not visible. The following games provide the basis for developing a new kind of sensory awareness. They help players isolate and examine the individual senses. They also suggest ways in which players may begin to realize that, in a manner of speaking, *they* are detached from their senses.

Count off into teams. Each player is to work individually on the problems while remaining a part of his or her team. Do not ask single individuals to perform during the first session. Security within the group is essential if the individual is to let go of fears.

Do not dwell on sensory problems too long. These games are only the first step in helping players to recognize that physical memory exists within them and can be called up intuitively without thinking, whenever needed.

☐ *Physical or sensory involvement with the environment can be firmly established in the player in early sessions. This is a necessary step on the path to building other and more complex relations.*

☐ *The intuitive bypasses the intellect, the mind, the memory, and the known. Players need not withdraw into a subjective world, they need not drift into a cloud of memories when working/ playing in the theater or the classroom.*

Ideas, terms, and phrases important to this chapter:

Subjectivity: Self-involvement, an inability to make contact with the environment and let it show itself. A player who is too subjective has difficulty in playing with others.

Listening/hearing: Hearing is the neglected part of listening. Hearing puts the responsibility for listening on the one who wants/needs to be heard.

Looking/seeing: A tree is a tree before you thought you could see the tree.

Sending and receiving: The artist, actor, and dancer use the body as instrument. Why not the student and teacher as well? Look/see through the eye (instrument); do not become the eye. Listen/hear through the ear (instrument), not with it (ear). Internal/external phenomena can then be seen, heard, felt, and acted upon simultaneously.

You stay out of it!: Stops the self from interfering and controlling.

SINGLE FILE ★

Purpose: To encourage players to pay attention to stage action.

Focus: On observing and remembering.

Description: Five or more players are chosen to go from the room and run back in, one behind another in a line, and out again. All other players watch closely. Players return out of formation. Audience players then rearrange runners, putting them back in their original order. When audience players agree that they have runners back in original order, runners make any necessary corrections.

Note: This is an excellent warm-up for any observation game.

—I SEE YOU ★

Description: Any number of couples stand in four lines. Players in each pair of lines face one another (that is, the x's face the o's). Those standing on the outside (the o's) play "peek-a-boo," looking at each other over their partner's left shoulder on "see" (bar 1) and over the right on "see" (bar 2). They repeat these movements rapidly through bars 3 and 4, slowly through bars 5 and 6, and rapidly again through bars 7 and 8.

    Those to the outside (the o's) clap on "If" (bar 9), polka or skip to the left of their own partners, meet midway between the lines, and, joining hands, swing twice round. Releasing hands, they clap on "If" (bar 13), return to own partners, join both hands, and swing twice round, finishing with the inside players (the x's) on the outside. With roles reversed, they repeat as before.

Notes: 1. This traditional children's game is Swedish in origin and appears in *Folk Games of Denmark and Sweden* by Dagny Pederson and Neva L. Boyd (Chicago: H.T. Fitz-Simons Co., Inc.).

    2. Try this delightful singing game as a warm-up to a workshop session on observation, using FEELING SELF WITH SELF, SENDING SIGHT OUT, and SEEING THROUGH OBJECTS.

o o o o o o

x x x x x x

    Eight feet between pairs of lines.

x x x x x x

o o o o o o

I see you I see you, Ti - ra la la la, la la la la la la! I see you I

see you Ti - ra la la la, la la la! If you see me then I see you

If you take me, then I take you; If you see me then I see you; If you take me I take you.

— When I Go to California ★ —

Purpose: To develop memory and observation.

Focus: On remembering a series in sequence.

Description: Teams of ten to twelve players in a circle.

Part 1. (The traditional game When I Go to California): The first player says, "When I go to California, I'm going to take a *trunk* (or any other object)." The second says, "When I go to California, I'm going to take a trunk and a *hat box*." The third player takes a trunk and a hat box and adds something new. Each player takes, *in exact order*, all that has gone before and adds a new object. If a player makes a mistake, that player cannot add an object and sits out until only one player is left.

Part 2. (The traditional game When My Ship Comes In): Same team plays as above, but instead of saying "take my shoes," for example, player acts out putting on shoes. Therefore, there is no speech in this game, only action. The next player repeats the first player's acting out and adds a new one. Thus player will put on shoes and perhaps play a flute. Each player repeats, in order, all that has gone before and adds a new bit of action.

Part 3. Same team plays again as in Part 1, but with a new series of objects. This time, however, players take time to *see* each object as they listen.

Notes: 1. In Part 1 a player often will be able to remember every object or act in the series but, almost unbelievably, forgets the very last object named. Such a player has probably cut off his attention to the last player in order to pre-plan the object or act to be added.

2. However, when objects are acted out, players rarely forget preceding objects. Repeating Part 1 while *seeing* the objects named eases remembering for players.

Part 2:
Give objects their place in space!
Keep objects in space — out of head!

Part 3:
(As fellow players add new objects):
Take time to see the objects!
See the objects as they are added!

Did you see *the word as it was spoken?*

— BLACK MAGIC ★ —————————————————

Purpose: To make players aware of the many properties of objects.

Description: Only two players should be told how the game works. One of them is sent from the room while the group decides on an object. That player is then called back in. The other player asks the first to say whether the selected object is a certain book, the clock, or any other object. Immediately before naming the selected object, he or she names something that is black in color. That indicates to the first player that the next object named is the one the group selected. The other players try to discover how the trick is done. The game can be repeated, even after the other players understand the basic trick, by having two partners decide privately what the characteristic of the clue object will be (it could have four legs, be made of paper, be electrical, or whatever). The nature of the clue object must not change, although the specific clue object should change, until the group correctly guesses what characteristic provided the clue. (That is, for example, the clue object may be a chair, a table, or a dog — all of them four-legged.)

—— EGYPTIAN WRITING ★ ————————————

Purpose: To sharpen players' acuteness of observation.

Description: Two players (a "magician" and a "reader")
who know the trick cooperate. The reader goes from the
room while the group agrees upon a word, for instance,
chair. The reader is called in and the magician, who has
a wand, spells out the word starting sentences with the
consonants of the word and tapping a code for the vowels
with the wand, all the while pretending to be "writing"
in the air. (Tapping for the vowels is as follows: one tap
is for *a*, two for *e*, three for *i*, four for *o*, five for *u*.) In
spelling *chair*, the magician may start off as follows:
"Carefully observe every stroke, now." (This provides the
c in *chair*.) The magician then writes in the air or on the
floor and says, "Have you got that?" He or she then taps
the floor once for the letter *a*, writes again, taps the floor
three times for *i*, writes again and says, "Rather complicated but you are a talented reader." The reader of Egyptian
writing says, "Chair." The other players try to discover
the trick. (Many students may volunteer to play reader
though they haven't understood the system. Discourage
false attempts as they will only confuse the class.)

—— THREE CHANGES ★ ————————————————

Purpose: To improve players' powers of observing.

Focus: On other player to see where changes were made.

Description: Full group counts off into teams of two
players each. All teams play simultaneously. Partners observe one another, noting dress, hair, accessories, and so
on. Partners then turn backs on each other and each makes
three changes in personal appearance: they part hair, untie
a shoelace, switch watch to the other arm, etc. When
ready, partners again face each other and each tries to
identify what changes the other has made.

Notes: 1. By changing partners and asking for four changes,
this game can be played with excitement for some time.

2. Change partners again and ask for five, six, seven,
and even eight changes, observing the back for changes
as well.

3. This leads right into the Mirror games (see Chapter 8).

— OBSERVATION GAME ★ ———————

Purpose: To improve memory.

Focus: On fully and carefully observing a set of objects.

Description: Any number of players. A dozen or more real objects are placed on a tray which is set in the center of a circle of players. After ten or fifteen seconds, the tray is covered or removed. Players then write individual lists naming as many of the objects as can be remembered. The lists are then compared with the tray of objects.

Notes: 1. Depending on the age of your group, add to or decrease the number of objects called for in the description.

2. Of course, this game is also useful in developing study skills.

— WHO STARTED THE MOTION? ★ ———

Purpose: To view others critically.

Focus: On trying to keep the center player from finding the leader who starts the motion.

Description: Players stand in a circle. One player is sent from the room while another player is selected to be the leader who starts the motion. The outside player is called back, stands in the center of the circle, and tries to discover the leader who is leading the other players through different motions (moving hands, tapping feet, nodding heads, etc.). Leader may change motions at any time, sometimes even when the center player is looking directly at the leader. When the center player discovers the leader, two other players are chosen to take their places.

Notes: 1. This traditional game is an excellent warm-up to the Mirror games, following, for it requires careful viewing of fellow players.

2. Immediately after playing this game, you may have players count off into teams of two for THREE CHANGES, which also leads into the Mirror games.

(Only if leader does not change the motion often enough):
Leader, change your movement when you get a chance! Watch for the change, other players, without giving the leader away!

SENDING SIGHT OUT

Purpose: To develop the sense of sight.

Focus: On seeing as a physical extension of the eyes.

Description: Players send their sight out to observe objects and allow objects to be seen.

Variation: Players are sidecoached to extend their sight in different directions without turning their heads. They thus explore their peripheral vision.

Notes: 1. The eyes are part of the physical body, and vision is a physical antenna (extension) reaching beyond the body into the environment.

    2. In classical Greek science there was a theory (Plato discusses it) that sight exists because of many tiny rays which extend from our eyes into the world.

    3. FEELING SELF WITH SELF is an excellent lead-in to this game.

    4. This is another game players can practice on their own.

Send your sight out into the environment!
Your sight is a physical extension of you!
Let your sight be active!
Send your sight out into the middle of the room!
All around you!
Allow an object to come in and be seen!
Take time to see that object!
The moment you see an object, let that object see you!
Keep changing objects!

Variation:
Turn your eyes to the left as far as possible!
Farther!
Now to the right!
Don't turn your head, just turn your eyes.
Try to see behind you!
Now look straight forward but see left! Right!
Now look up as far as you can!
Down!
Repeat!

What is the difference between seeing an object and letting an object be seen?
Can you answer this?

— SEEING THROUGH OBJECTS ——————

Purpose: To understand seeing in a new way.

Focus: On looking through an object.

Description: Players send their sight out as if it were a force which could go through a solid object and return.

Notes: 1. Have players send their sight through a set of windowpanes (out one pane, back through another) to clarify this exercise.

2. SENDING SIGHT OUT is a good warm-up for this game.

3. More advanced students may want to have explained to them the differences between X-rays, radar, and human sight.

Send your sight out!
Let sight go through things!
Send it through things and let it return!
You are not trying to see!
You are at rest!
Look through something, not at it!

Players, did this make looking seem different!

— SEEING A SPORT: RECALL ——————

Purpose: To help players recognize the vastness and availability of past experience.

Focus: On recalling the colors, sounds, movements, characters, etc. of a past experience.

Description: All sit quietly and recall a time when they were present at a sports event.

Notes: 1. "Seeing" homework: Tell players to take a few moments out of each day to focus on what is around, noticing colors, sounds, observing the environment, etc.

2. This game is a valuable lead-in to the *Where* games.

3. The Stanislavski "method" of teaching acting, which has been so influential in the United States and the Soviet Union, encourages performers to recall "sense memories" of events and feelings in their own lives, and to relate those memories to the characters they are playing. This approach has dominated our "serious" theater for the past half-century.

Focus on colors!
Listen for sounds!
Focus on odors!
See movement!
Now put them all together!
Focus on what's above, below, all around you!
Focus on your self!

Did the past come into the present!

—— Listening to the Environment ————

Purpose: To develop and appreciate the sense of hearing.

Focus: On hearing as many sounds as possible in the immediate environment.

Description: Whole group sits quietly with eyes closed for one minute or so and listens to the sounds of the immediate environment. Players take note of how many different sounds there are in the environment.

Notes: 1. Assign this exercise as homework to be done a few minutes each day while walking, at home, with the family, etc.

2. Remind players of how much of the world they understand through hearing and suggest that they try to imagine what the world is like for those who cannot hear.

Hear all the sounds around you —
whether the faintest of faint or the
most deafening!
Listen!
Hear as many sounds as possible!

What sounds did you hear?
(Have players identify as many
sounds as possible.)
How many heard that sound?
Any sounds not mentioned yet?

—— Sending Hearing Out ——————

Purpose: To extend players' understanding of their hearing.

Focus: On hearing sounds (without attitudes toward them).

Description: Players hear the sounds in the environment and let the sounds be heard.

Notes: 1. This exercise can be done while sitting at desks, or at any time of the day.

2. If done with some regularity, this exercise may bring more texture to sound.

3. Different nerve endings in the ear respond to different pitches. It is apparently possible, therefore, for the ears to "tune" themselves to hear a certain pitch or kind of sound. Students with some musical training may appreciate an analogy between the eardrum and the sympathetic strings on musical instruments like the sitar, which vibrate when the same note is sounded by another string.

Send your hearing out into the
world above, behind, below, near
and far from you!
Your hearing is a part of you!
Your antenna!
Your scout!
Send your hearing out into
the space!
Pick up the sounds you find there!
Let your hearing pick up
the sounds!
You stay out of it!
Let the sounds be heard!

(Discuss hearing as a physical
antenna extending a great
distance from the physical body.)

Chapter 7:
PART OF A WHOLE GAMES

Linking the Players

Becoming or being part of a whole produces one body through which all (onstage players, audience players, and sidecoach) are directly involved in the outcome of the playing, supporting one another in a process of mutual fulfillment. A player with body, mind, and intuition functioning in unison at top levels of personal, individual energy connects with fellow players in an effort to break out of past limitations. One player thus supported by many is free to play, and the many thus act as one. Effort and the resulting breakthrough (if accomplished) are shared equally by all as part of the whole.

□ Competition and comparisons that fragment a person and isolate one player from fellow players destroy part of the whole.

When a player realizes he or she cannot play tag without someone to tag him or her, or when a baseball team can look at another team not as the opposition, but as fellow players, then both teams become part of the whole (in harmony), giving and taking towards mutual fulfillment — playing!

Contests for breaking existing records — in sports, music, or whatever — should be entered into for the sheer pleasure, exhilaration, and elation inherent with extension (a plant reaching for the sun, a man stepping on the moon). A breakthrough for one becomes a breakthrough for all.

□ Take care not to encourage competition by dispensing rewards to "good" players and punishment to "bad" ones.

Responsiveness, interaction, attention, observation, physical and vocal expression, narrative skills, sensory agility, emotional awareness, and more will develop more swiftly when students become part of the whole.

Ideas, terms, and phrases important to this chapter:

Freedom: A discovery, made in workshops when players, as part of the whole, recognize existing limits and accept their right to explore the possibility of breaking through.

Community (harmony, unity): A phenomenon of the spirit which enters the classroom environment, releasing individual response, a sense of self-worth, joyous laughter, as individuals make personal contributions to mutual problem solving.

Show, don't tell!: Aims at helping players physicalize objects, involvements, relationships without imposing themselves. The goal is a *subjective* communication.

Share your voice!: Produces projection, responsibility to the audience.

PART OF A WHOLE, OBJECT

Purpose: To make players interdependent.

Focus: On becoming part of a larger object.

Description: One player enters the playing area and becomes part of a large object or organism (animal, vegetable, or mineral). Examples include a machine, clockworks, abstract mechanisms, animals, natural elements. As soon as the nature of the object becomes clear to another player, he or she joins as part of the whole. Play continues until all are participating and working together to form the complete object. Players may assume any movement, sound, or position to help complete the whole.

Notes: 1. This game is useful as a warm-up or as a close to a session, as it generates spontaneity and energy. Players often stray from the original "idea" of the first player, resulting in fanciful abstraction.

2. The teacher should use sidecoaching to help single players join in, those who fear they may be guessing wrong about the object that is forming, or those who rush to join in without awareness of the whole.

3. This theater game is also widely played under the name MACHINE.

Use your whole body to become your part!
Join in!
Be brave!
Change!
Become another part of the object!
There are no right answers!

What was the whole object?
What did you think it was before you joined?

— PART OF A WHOLE, ACTIVITY ——————

Purpose: To collaborate in stage activity.

Focus: On showing a whole general activity by taking a part in it.

Description: Large teams of ten to fifteen players. Players agree on first player, who secretly chooses a group project and begins an activity related to it. When the nature of the whole general activity becomes apparent, other players join in, one at a time, and take a part in the project. An example is planting a garden: first player rakes leaves into piles, second player hoes, third fertilizes, etc.

Notes: 1. This group interaction should create flow and energy. Repeat the game until this takes place or end it if this does not happen.

2. Players are *not* to know ahead of time what the first player is doing.

3. Players reluctant to take part for fear of being "wrong" about the project can be comforted to find during the evaluation period that many players had differing ideas.

4. Even if the playing area is chaotic, with everyone moving and talking at once, refrain from trying to get an orderly scene. Early pleasure and excitement in play is essential to the social growth of the group.

5. PLAYGROUND is a good lead-in to this game.

Show!
Don't tell!
Avoid dialogue!
Other players, give yourself time
to see what's going on!
Take a risk!
Join the activity!
Become part of the whole!

What was the group activity?
Players, were you part of
the whole?
Were there other activities possible
in the project?
Were the objects in the space?
Audience, do you agree with
players?

—— PART OF A WHOLE, OCCUPATION ——

Purpose: To define a character through characteristic behavior.

Focus: On becoming part of a whole occupational activity.

Description: Teams of five or six players agree on a first player, who secretly decides on an occupation and starts an activity related to it. Other players join in one at a time as definite characters (the *Who*) and begin or join in an activity related to the occupation. For example, first player washes hands, stands waiting with hands in air, second player becomes a nurse, enters playing area to help doctor put on gloves. Other players become anesthetist, patient, intern.

Notes: 1. Players are not to know ahead of time what the first player is doing or who he or she is.

2. If the players become too verbal or move around aimlessly, focus is not complete. Call time or go on to another game.

3. Even though the *Who* is added here, take care that focus is kept on the activity or players will begin to "act."

4. If students have difficulty relating to an activity, point out that members of different professions have different attitudes and interests. Doctors, writers, plumbers, deliverymen, custodial workers, real estate salesmen will enter the same room looking at different things and demonstrating different interests.

Show!
Don't tell!
Join the activity as a definite character!
Become part of the whole!
Show through activity!
(If dialogue emerges):
Share your voice!

Audience, what was the occupation?
Did players show or tell?
Players, do you agree?
Before joining in, what did each player think the occupation was?
Audience, did you have different ideas of what was happening?

— PART OF A WHOLE, RELATIONSHIP ——————

Purpose: To define a character through human context.

Focus: On communicating *Who* (relationship) through an activity.

Description: Count off into teams of five or more. One player begins a simple activity without choosing a character. Other players choose a character relationship with the onstage player and, one at a time, join the activity. The first player must accept and relate to any incoming players as if the relationships were known.

Example: Man hangs a picture; woman enters saying she would like the picture hung higher. Man accepts her as his wife and continues hanging picture. Other players come in as their children, neighbors, etc. All show relationship through activity.

Notes: 1. This game will bring forth first signs of an event (scene) emerging from the focus (or first signs of the relationship) rather than mere simultaneous activity.

2. Refrain from trying to get an orderly scene. ROCKING THE BOAT/SHARING THE STAGE PICTURE will help clear chaotic stages.

Show! Don't tell!
Stay with the activities!
No guessing!
No need to rush!
Let who you are be discovered through activity!
When you know who you are, show us through playing!
(If dialogue emerges):
Share your voice!
Let who you are be revealed through the activity!

Audience, who were players?
What were the relationships?
Did players show us through activity?
When you entered the activity, players, did you know who you were?
What is the most typical thing done by your best friend?
What habits can you see in your favorite TV characters?
Do you ever imitate your family or people you admire?
Do you know families whose members all do things the same way?

Chapter 8:
MIRROR GAMES

Reflecting and Sharing What Is Observed

Mirror games link players by the act of seeing. Players are on focus when they merely reflect, without interpretation, what their eyes tell them. And so, sidecoaching for this and other Mirror games is, **Reflect what you see, not what you think you see! Keep the mirror between you!**

The games call for spontaneous reflection, not imitation. This subtle but essential difference must be observed for Mirror games to be effective. Mirror reflection requires a nonverbal, noncerebral response.

□ *Reflection is to act. Imitation is to react.*

In imitation, what is seen is sent through the head for analysis before it is shared. This creates a time lag. That time lag is the space through which theories and prejudices enter and dissipate the spontaneous moment. In true reflection, time lag is eliminated. There is not time for thinking about playing — the player acts instinctively.

□ *Good imitation — like that of actors who do impressions of celebrities — is a remarkable skill, but limited and limiting.*

An important discovery is made through FOLLOW THE FOLLOWER (below), the most advanced of the Mirror games. When following the follower, players move in accord with one another but there is no leader. All players lead. No one initiates. All initiate. All reflect. Communication among players is so strong it is difficult to see where the movement begins. Players experience something like collective consciousness.

□ *Even in these games, many students may want to "act." Remind them that without another player there is no game. One cannot even play tag if there is no one to tag.*

You are on your own! Do not initiate! Follow the initiator! Follow the follower! are sidecoaching phrases for this series of games. Seeing a continuous reflecting of oneself as reflected by another player brings about a flowing movement and change without anyone deliberately initiating: one is simply reflecting what one sees.

Bring this point home. When you see a player initiate a movement during FOLLOW THE FOLLOWER, ask that player, "Did you *see* that movement? Or are you initiating?" If played frequently, varying partners often, FOLLOW THE FOLLOWER can bring miraculous unity and harmony to a classroom. When players see themselves working together there is a moment of awe, joy, and laughter. The playing area is filled with a flowing movement and change. Players recognize that they are intertwined with one

□ FOLLOW THE FOLLOWER *quiets the mind and frees the players to enter a common time and space.*

another in a nonphysical, nonverbal, nonpsychological, nonanalytical, nonjudgmental area of their free inner selves.

The shared discoveries about human interaction which are made in FOLLOW THE FOLLOWER are similar to those found in many other theater games.

Ideas, terms, and phrases important to this chapter:

Imitation: A skill but a limiting one, an obstacle in our search for spontaneity.

Reflection: Organic action directly upon what is seen. (For the distinction between action and reaction see the following chapters.) It makes players alive and alert in the present moment. (It is best not to discuss these differences, but to let students make the discoveries themselves.)

Camera!: Encourages the player to think of himself or herself as a single lens or eye from head to toe. Explains full-body concentration.

Follow the follower!: (See the text above.)

— ADAM'S SONS★ ———————————————

Description: Children form a circle, hands joined, one in the center. All march and sing. On "now all do this" all stop marching and imitate the one in center, who shows various activities, such as washing the clothes, sawing the wood, threshing the wheat, etc. On "said Adam" all bow, i.e., bob the head quickly to the player in the center. That player then chooses a replacement and the game is played again, alternating verses.

Ad - am had sev - en sons, sev - en sons, sev - en sons had Ad - am. All the sons were hap - py and glad,
And Eve had sev - en sons, sev - en sons, sev - en sons had E - ve. All the sons were hap - py and glad,

And all did what Ad - am said. "Now all do this, now all do that, now all do this, now all do that," said Ad - am.
And all did what E - ve said. "Now all do this, now all do that, now all do this, now all do that," said E - ve.

— MIRROR ——————————————————————

Purpose: To help players see with the full body; to reflect, not imitate, the other.

Focus: On exact mirror-image reflection of the initiator's movements.

Description: Players count off into teams of two players. One player becomes A, the other B. All teams play simultaneously. A faces B. Explain that B is a person looking in a mirror. A is that person's image in the mirror. A reflects all movements initiated by B, head to foot, including facial expressions. After a time, positions are reversed so that B reflects A.

Notes 1. Watch for assumptions, which prevent reflection. For example, if B makes a familiar movement, does A anticipate and assume the next move, or does A stay with B?

2. Watch for true reflection. If B uses right hand, does A use right hand or opposite hand? Do not bring this aspect of the game to players' attention cerebrally. Playing WHO IS THE MIRROR? (following) will bring an organic understanding of reflection.

3. Changeover or reverse should be made without stopping the flow of movement between players.

4. THREE CHANGES is an ideal warm-up for this game.

B, start moving!
A, reflect!
Big full-body movements!
Reflect only what you see! Not what you think you see!
Keep the mirror between you!
Reflect fully — head to toe!
Change!
Now A start movement and B reflect!
Know when you start movements!
Know when you start mirroring!
Change! . . . Change! . . .

Do members of groups (families, school groups, nationalities) imitate one another?

— WHO IS THE MIRROR? ——————————

Purpose: To prepare for FOLLOW THE FOLLOWER.

Focus: On concealing from audience which player is the mirror.

Description: Teams of two, with an audience. Before "calling curtain," players decide which player will be the initiator and which the mirror. This game is played in exactly the same way as MIRROR, except that the teacher does not call out *Change!* One player initiates all movement, the other reflects, and both players attempt to conceal which one is the mirror from the audience players. When the two players are moving, the teacher calls out the name of one player. Audience members raise hands if that player appears to be the mirror. Teacher then calls out the name of the other player for audience hands. Both players continue playing during the voting without stopping, until the vote is unanimous for one or the other player or until stalemate is reached.

(To audience):
Which player is the mirror?

—— FOLLOW THE FOLLOWER ——————

Purpose: To give players a sense of themselves and their union with others through reflection.

Focus: On following the follower.

Description: Teams of two, with an audience. One player becomes the mirror image of the other, the initiator. Teacher will start the players playing MIRROR, calling **Change!** at intervals for players to reverse roles. When players are initiating and reflecting with full-body movements, call, **On your own!** Players then immediately begin reflecting each other without either one knowing who is initiating movement.

Notes: 1. Start players on their own only when they are in full-body motion. This will ensure that the mirror has something to observe/reflect.

  2. This is tricky — players are not to initiate but are to follow the initiator. Both are at once the initiator and the mirror. Players reflect themselves being reflected.

Reflect!
Reflect only what you see — not what you think you will see!
Change!

(Teacher may enter the playing area to check player initiations.)

Use your whole body!
You are on your own!
Follow the follower!
Keep the mirror between you!
Follow the follower!

(During actual play, to a moving player):
Did you start that movement?
Or did you reflect what you saw?
Audience, do you agree with this player?

Chapter 9:
WHERE, WHO, AND *WHAT*

Creating Environments, Characters, and Action through Play

The terms *Where, Who,* and *What* are used as nouns in the description of many theater games. These broad and neutral terms are particularly useful in the schoolroom. The terms "set," "character," and "stage action" limit discussion among players to the theater situation.

☐ *Using the terms* Where, Who, *and* What *moves the players to include environment, relationship, and activity — the world of daily living — in their consideration of theatrical problems.*

Where Games (Setting/Environment)

Prior to presenting the Where games, hold a discussion with the group along the following lines:

"How do you know where you are?" If you get no response, try a different approach.

"Is it true that you always know where you are?"

"No. Sometimes you don't know where you are."

"True, you may be in an unfamiliar place. How do you know it's unfamiliar? How do you know when you are in a familiar place? How do you know where you are at any moment of the day?"

"You just know." "You can tell." "There are signs."

"How do you know you are in the kitchen?"

"You can smell the cooking."

"If there were nothing cooking, how would you know?"

"By where it is."

"What do you mean?"

"By where it is in the house."

"If every room in the house were moved around, would you still know which room was the kitchen?"

"Of course!"

"How?"

"By the things in the room."

"What things?"

"The stove." "The refrigerator."

"Would you know a kitchen if it had no stove or refrigerator in it? If it were in the jungle, for instance?"

"Yes."

"How?"

"It would be a place where they get food ready."

And so, through examples, discussion, answering of detailed questions, the players conclude that, "We know where we are by the physical objects around us."

When this basic premise has been agreed upon, become more specific:

"What is the difference between an office and a den?"

"An office has a desk and a telephone."

"Isn't this also true of most dens? What might a den have that an office would not have?"

"Photographs, rugs, lamps."

"Couldn't these be in an office?"

On a blackboard, set up two columns under the headings of den and office. Now ask the group to call out items which might be found in each place, listing each under the proper heading.

Eventually, it will become apparent that differences do exist; while both locations might have a desk or a water cooler, one is more likely to find a copying machine or intercom system in an office than in a den.

Continue along this same line: "How do you know the difference between a park and a garden?" The more detailed these discussions become, the more students will realize that the definition of *Where* is an exciting issue in playmaking. (The demonstration which precedes the Where games should make the idea even clearer.)

Who Games (Character/Relationship)

In a similar manner, introduce *Who.*

"Do you usually know the person in the same room with you? Would you know a stranger from your brother? Your uncle from the corner grocer?"

"Of course."

"Can you tell the difference between two school friends and two strangers and two people who have just met?"

"Yes."

"How can you tell?"

"By the way they act together."

"What do you mean, 'by the way they act together'?"

"Friends don't stop talking." "Strangers pretend they don't notice one another." "People who just met are polite."

In discussion, students will agree that people show us who they are not by what they say about themselves but through their behavior. When they have arrived at this point, bring up the fact that actors, to communicate their identities to the audience, must show *Who* through relationships with their fellow players.

Show! Don't tell! will bring a deeper understanding of how, every day, we reveal ourselves to one another, without saying a word.

☐ *The use of* Who *games during theater-game workshops will open players to a clearer observation of their human world.*

What Games (Action)

Discuss, in much the same way:
"Why do you usually go into a kitchen?"
"To make a sandwich." "To get a glass of water." "To wash the dishes."
"Why do you go into a bedroom?"
"To sleep." "To change clothes."
"The living room?"
"To read." "To watch TV."
As questioning progresses, players will agree that we usually have a need for being where we are and for doing what we do — for handling certain physical objects, for going into certain places or rooms. And so must the onstage player have a need for handling certain props, for being a certain place, for acting a certain way in the playing area.

☐ *Stage action* (What) *is the interaction of character with character, character with setting.*

Do not confuse deciding upon *What* with preplanning the plot or story line before playing the theater games. If baseball players knew ahead of time which pitches were going to be strikes and which were going to be hit out of the ballpark, all the fun (the story) would be taken out of the game. *Where, Who,* and *What* simply lay out the field upon which the game is played. For instance, in baseball, the *Where* is the diamond, the foul lines, the bases, and also the bat, ball, gloves, etc.; the *Who* is the first baseman, pitcher, batter, catcher, etc., and *What* is the game's activities — running bases, catching balls, etc.

In baseball the focus of the game is simply to "keep your eye on the ball." As was observed in Chapter 1, the focus of a theater game is similar, not an end in itself but a means to an end. In *Where, Who,* and *What* games, staying on focus provides the energy needed for playing.

☐ *The energy of a game flows through the form —the* Where, Who, *and* What *— to shape the real-life event that is happening onstage — the story.*

Ideas, terms, and phrases important to this chapter:

Action: Reaching out to, intersecting with the environment, including the human environment (which in turn acts upon the player). Action creates process and change and makes possible the building of a scene.

Reaction: A self-protective withdrawal from the environment.

Playwriting (planning how): *No playwriting!* is a sidecoaching phrase which, when used during play, brings players out from behind words to join in the events in process. If players stay on focus, the problem will be resolved without planning. (The discussion of the writing of plays is reserved for a later chapter.)

***Keep your eye on the ball! Your fellow player! Your prop!*:** Anchors the play in movement and prevents pre-planning.

***Show! Don't tell!*:** Showing is physical. Telling is only talking about what is happening.

Where Games, Demonstration

Students familiar with space substance should not find it difficult to understand *Where,* but a demonstration will probably be useful.

Place a chair in the playing area and proceed as follows, using your own words: "You all know that a chair, being solid (lift it up), visible (turn it around), and made of a particular substance (knock on it), requires that we pay attention to it. We can see this chair! Even if we could *not* see this chair, we could not walk through it (demonstrate). The chair takes up space." Sit on the chair: "Is this chair in the space or in my head?" The answer will be obvious. "Have there been times when a chair was in your head and not in the space you thought it occupied? Have you ever missed the chair when sitting down and fallen on the floor?" Many players will have seen or felt this experience. Except for real chairs used for sitting, all objects needed for a theater game will be made of space substance. All players respect the (invisible) space a space object occupies as they would a real object. "Remember, ***Keep objects in the space and out of the head!***"

As an example, demonstrate space objects. Walk to a

☐ *Until we have learned how to levitate, real chairs or benches must be used for couches, beds, and actual chairs in theater games. However, to help preserve the focus of all players, we suggest that beds be but one chair rather than a row of chairs. A chair can become a bed if one stretches out one's legs, turns on a space-substance reading lamp, pulls up space-substance covers, etc.*

☐ *Playing* RELAY WHERE *(below) will also help to introduce the* Where.

desk (made of space), open a drawer in the desk, and take out a pencil (space). Write on a piece of paper on top of the desk. Move to a window (space) and open it, etc. After each object is used, ask students, "Was the object in space or just an idea in my head?"

If you prefer, ask two students to do this demonstration. A sets up an object; B uses it. B sets up an object; A uses it. After each set-up ask, "Was the object in their heads or in the space?" Use of the space objects will reveal that space objects take up as much space as real objects.

— Dog & Bone★ ——————————————————

Purpose: To bring all players into the same working space.

Focus: Dog: on hearing; players: on being silent. The object of the game is to become and to remain the dog.

Description: All the players, with the exception of one—the dog—sit on the floor in a circle. The dog sits or lies on the floor in the center of the circle with eyes shut and with a bone (any object) within arm's reach. One of the players (the mastermind) silently signals another one to steal the bone. If the thief can get the bone and return to place without being heard by the dog, he or she becomes the dog; if not, the dog continues until the bone is successfully stolen. Should the dog hear the thief he or she must point in the direction of the noise; and the thief, if detected, returns to place while another thief is chosen.

Variation: When the thief returns to the circle with the bone, he or she holds it behind the back. The dog is told to open eyes and is given one chance to guess the identity of the thief. If successful, the dog remains dog. If not, the thief becomes the dog.

Notes: 1. If one player successfully steals the bone but does not want to become the dog, have that player select another in his or her place. In time, the shy player will join the others in wanting to become the dog.

2. This game provides full participation, total body involvement, and a great deal of excitement in a class.

3. This is one of a number of excellent games collected by Neva Boyd in her *Handbook of Games.*

Was the dog focusing on hearing?
Or was the dog guessing?

— Airport ★

Purpose: To encourage players to collaborate in the creation of a *Where.*

Description: Masking tape or chalk is used to outline a rectangle approximately 4 feet by 12 feet. This represents an airport landing strip. Objects of various sizes (books, boxes, cans, chalkboard erasers, shoes, etc.) are placed randomly in this area.

Players count off into groups of two. (One blindfold is needed for each pair.) One player is the pilot, who stands at one end of the rectangle; the other player is the "control tower" at the opposite end of the rectangle. Because of poor visibility, the tower must guide the pilot to a safe landing at the end of the runway nearest the tower. To play, the pilot is blindfolded and now must rely on the tower to get through obstacles. To make a safe landing, the pilot must not touch or knock over any object or step out of the rectangle. The tower guides the pilot by calling out, "Left foot — slide forward. Stop! Right foot — step right. Stop. Lift left foot high — higher — now forward — a little more — put it down," and the like. The game is over when an obstacle is knocked over or the pilot steps out of the rectangle, or has avoided all objects and steps out the far end. Several rectangles can be set up and used by several teams at the same time.

Note: For players who are not yet clear on left and right, make small four-inch squares of cardboard, half of them covered with sandpaper, the rest smooth. One smooth square and one with sandpaper is given to each pilot and tower. (The sandpaper is held in the right hand, say, and the smooth square in the left.) The tower then calls, "Sandpaper foot forward! Smooth paper tiny step . . ." etc. Doing this can help young players distinguish between right and left.

— WHERE GAME WITH DIAGRAMS ——————

Purpose: To make the invisible visible.

Focus: On showing where you are by making physical contact with all the objects drawn on a floor plan. To show *Where*. Each player must in some way handle or touch everything drawn on the floor plan, sharing with the audience its visibility.

Description: Teams of two. Each team of two is supplied with blackboard and chalk (or paper and pencils). They then agree on a place (*Where*) and plot out a floor plan. (If the team chooses a living room, they will plot out the sofa, chairs, coffee table, fireplace, rug, pictures, windows, doors, etc.). Encourage each player to contribute a share of the items, using the standard floorplan symbols. (See illustrations.) Then have players walk through the playing area, making contact with all elements of the floor plan, which are space objects. The only physical objects on the stage will be chairs. Players may improvise dialogue or perform a scene from a play. They may also do a scene in gibberish.

Notes: 1. The floor plan must face the stage where the onstage players can see it.

    2. The players are not to remember any of the items but refer to the floor plan as often as they wish during the exercise. This is a deliberate step to ease players from remembering (blanking the mind) and will give a great sense of relief if stressed. It is another step in helping the player relax the cerebral hold.

    3. As much as possible, let the cast members discover variations for themselves.

    4. Artists and architects must do much of this sort of planning before construction begins. This game, by making planning fun in itself, will encourage students to take time to design carefully their classroom projects.

Look at your floor plan!
Out of your head — into the space!

Did players keep their focus?
Could objects have been used in a less ordinary manner?
Are hands the only way of touching objects?
(Objects can be fallen against, leaned on, etc. Noses can be pressed against windows as easily as hands can open them.)
Did players share what they were doing with us?

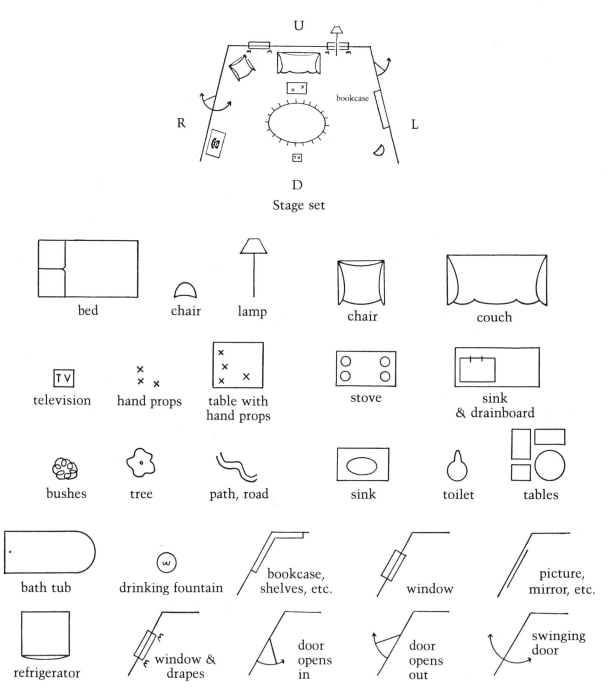

Stage set

bookcase

Suggested floorplan symbols

bed

chair

lamp

chair

couch

television

hand props

table with
hand props

stove

sink
& drainboard

bushes

tree

path, road

sink

toilet

tables

bath tub

drinking fountain

bookcase,
shelves, etc.

window

picture,
mirror, etc.

refrigerator

window &
drapes

door
opens
in

door
opens
out

swinging
door

— WHERE GAME WITH PROPS —

Purpose: To show players how a place can be defined by the people who occupy it and what they are doing.

Focus: On showing *Where*.

Description: Two teams. One team becomes audience. One player goes on stage and shows *Where* through physical use of objects. The first player to whom *Where* has been communicated assumes a *Who*, enters the *Where*, and develops a relationship (role) with the *Where* and the other player. Other players join them as related characters *(Who)* in the *Where* and the general activity *(What)*.

Example: Player goes on stage and shows the audience rows and rows of bookshelves. A second player enters, stands behind a counter, and begins removing and stamping cards from the inside covers of books. Third player enters, pushes cart to shelves, and begins stacking books. Other players enter the library *Where*.

*Keep focus on **Where!***
Relate to fellow players!
Keep in touch with the objects!

— EXCHANGING WHERES —

Purpose: To improvise on a situation without pre-planning.

Focus: On communicating *Where, Who,* and *What* without forethought.

Description: Divide group into teams of two to four players in such a way that the sexes are equally distributed among all teams. (For instance, each team might have one boy and two girls.) Each team agrees on *Where, Who,* and *What* and draws a floor plan of the *Where*, noting on it *Who* and *What*, the time of day, weather, etc. Teacher collects all floor plans and redistributes them, one by one, only when a team arrives in the playing area for its turn. No team is to get its own floor plan to work from. Players quickly look at the floor plan, decide quietly which players will be *Who*, and, without further discussion, enter the event (scene) designated by the floor plan, which should be kept at hand.

Notes: 1. This game alleviates the tendency to plan in advance.

2. Students might be asked what you can learn from a room about the people who live there.

Check the floor plan as you play!
Take your time!
*Communicate **Where!***
Don't tell!
Relate to each other through activity!
Objects!
Time of day!
Show!
Don't tell!

Audience, did players follow the floor plan?
Was the floor plan clear?
Did players show or tell?
Players, do you agree?
Did you let the new floor plan move you?
Or did you go back to your own team's first floor plan?

—— RELAY WHERE: BUILDING A SET ——————

Purpose: Making an invisible place visible using space objects.

Focus: On a chosen *Where* and all the objects within the *Where*.

Description: Count off into large teams of ten to fifteen players. Each team agrees on a *Where*. First player goes into the playing area and "finds" an object in the space that can be part of the chosen *Where* and leaves. Each successive player uses or makes contact with all the space objects already "found" and then adds another object related to the *Where*.

Example: First player finds a wash basin; second player washes hands and, using a towel, finds a rack. Next player opens a space-object door, and so on. Each player completes his or her task and exits before another player enters.

Note: Other settings for RELAY WHERE: train station, supermarket, airport, hospital waiting room, street scene, beach, schoolroom, art gallery, restaurant. Use a variety of settings for different locations, cultures, and periods.

First player, try not to decide ahead of time what your object will be!
*Focus on **Where**!*
Find the object in the stage space!
Fellow players, take time to see the onstage player's object appear!
Touch or use all previously placed objects!
*Use every object in the **Where**!*
What you need may appear!

Audience, where were they?
Were the objects in the space or in players' imaginations?
What about the (one of the objects that the players "found") — did all players touch or use the same object?
Players, do you agree with audience?

Would a father use a room differently from a mother?
Would a living room in Thomas Jefferson's house be the same as a living room in the White House today?

— WHAT TIME IS IT? —————————

Purpose: To establish setting and environment.

Focus: On feeling time with the whole body.

Description: Count off into two large teams. Working individually, within the team, players sit or stand, focusing on a time of day given by the teacher. Players may move only if pushed to do so by the focus but are not to bring in activity just to show time.

Notes: 1. Players are not to interact with one another during this exercise.

2. Each player will feel the time differently. For instance, 2:00 a.m. will mean sleep for many, but the night owl in the group will become wide awake.

3. Players are to add time to *Where, Who,* and *What* whenever possible, and time should be considered routinely as part of evaluation from now on.

4. In connection with the social-studies curriculum it is interesting to discuss the history of timepieces. Ask students, "If you lost your watch, how would you know the time? How did people used to tell time? Did the rich man or woman who owned a timepiece have power over those who didn't know the exact time of day?"

5. There are other interesting questions about time which are worth discussion: "How does a painter indicate the time of day in a painting? Do we always know the time of day in a work of art? Do we need to?"

Feel the time in your feet!
In your spine! In your legs!
No urgency!
Feel time on your face!
In your body!
Head to toe!
Allow the focus to work for you!

Is there bodily reaction to time?
Is it possible to communicate time
without activity or objects?
Did everyone feel the time in his
or her own way?
What were the differences?
Is clock time a cultural pattern?
Is there only sleep-time,
work-time, hungry-time?

EXPLORATION OF A LARGE ENVIRONMENT

Purpose: To discover a large environment inside a small space.

Focus: On relating to the larger, overall environment.

Description: Two or more players agree on a general large environment, such as a forest, mountain top, lake, etc., as *Where*. Players then agree on *Who* and *What* and explore the larger environment in space.

Notes: 1. Some players have difficulty moving out of the little details at hand in home, school, or office environments. Sidecoach players to see and communicate with what is beyond.

2. This game works well when connected with environmental studies.

What is above?
Beneath?
Beyond?
Communicate with the larger environment beyond you!
See the larger environment beyond!
Let it fill all the space in the room!
Let it go for miles around!

Audience, what was above players?
Beneath players?
Did players show or tell?
Players, do you agree?
Out of doors is the air different?
Can you breathe more freely in the country than in the city?
What might a scientist be doing in the forest? in the desert?

WHERE WITHOUT HANDS

Purpose: To define a setting with restricted movements.

Focus: On showing *Where* by contacting objects without using hands.

Description: A single player selects *Where, Who,* and *What*. For some reason player cannot or does not use hands but makes contact with objects in the environment to show *Where*.

Example: Player has fresh nail polish on, or is carrying a hot cake pan. This makes it necessary to open and shut drawers and closets with feet, elbows, and shoulders.

Notes: 1. Watch to see which players are breaking their dependency on the sidecoach, integrating use of "no hands" without need for sidecoaching.

2. Players who do not integrate the problem will keep focus on their hands instead of using objects to show *Where*, which completely alters the problem. Let the players discover this for themselves.

Know where you are!
Keep in contact with the total environment!
No hands!

What interesting ways of contacting objects were found?
Did Where *come to life?*

─── Showing Where without Objects ───

Purpose: To discover a variety of ways of indicating setting.

Focus: On showing *Where*.

Description: Players count off into teams of two or three. *Where*, *Who*, and *What* agreed upon. Players show *Where* without handling physical objects. Examples: tourists in a town square, young couple alone in a church, sailors standing watch on ship's bridge.

Notes: 1. Suggest that *Where* can be shown by any of the following: by looking at something (seeing); by hearing; by relationship (who you are); by sound; by lighting; through an activity.

2. By keeping focus on *Where* without being able to manipulate objects, players can learn to "feel" stage space. Players are in the *Where* from head to foot, so to speak.

3. Character relationships grow in intensity throughout this exercise.

4. Watch for fearful players who plan *Where* so that their actions are predetermined.

See where you are!
You are in it together!
Use all your senses!
Let where you are lead you through the event (scene)!
Take your time!
What's the weather like?

Did players show us or tell us?
Players, do you agree?
Did the Where *emerge from the focus?*
Audience, who were they?
Did this team benefit from previous teams' evaluations?

─── Where with Help ─────────────

Purpose: To work in teams to define a setting.

Focus: On physically helping fellow players make contact with every object in the *Where*.

Description: Teams of two players design a floor plan and agree on *Where*, *Who*, and *What*. Players help each other make contact with all the objects in the floor plan. Players are to integrate helping one another within the event (scene) without use of excessive dialogue.

Notes: 1. Tell players to add detail to their floor plans (map, pictures, props). Keep *What* very simple with no particular tension between players (they are watching television, washing dishes, etc.).

2. The game is over when all the objects have been contacted.

3. If time allows, let each team go through this game and the two following in one session.

Refer to the floor plan!
Help each other make contact!
Work on the problem!
Keep focus on physically helping!

Did players make contact with the objects through Where, Who *and* What, *or was contact random just for the sake of "touching the objects"?*
Did players physically help each other make contact?
Or did they rely on dialogue alone?

—— WHERE WITH OBSTACLES ——————————————

Purpose: To define a space by working *against* another player.

Focus: To hinder each other physically from making contact with every object in the *Where*.

Description: Same teams as in WHERE WITH HELP. *Where, Who,* and *What* agreed upon. Each player must contact every space object in the floor plan, at the same time physically trying to prevent the other from making contact with the same objects. There should be no excessive dialogue. Actions must be integrated; that is, one player cannot simply tackle another. He or she must hinder the second player while trying to do something appropriate to the space.

Notes: 1. This game and the one following (WHERE: HELP/HINDER) contain elements of physical conflict and should only be attempted with mature and responsible students.

2. Stress that players should integrate contact and obstacles with a minimum of dialogue.

3. If heightened actions and relationships are not evident, continue the game for more sessions.

4. Note that players must watch and involve themselves with each other most intently to solve the problem.

Hinder!
You must contact everything!
Make an obstacle to your
partner's move!
Hinder!
Avoid dialogue!
Make each contact make sense!

Did this exercise give Where *more visibility than the one before? Which gave* Who *more reality? Did players who made contact with objects make sense or did they dash around touching things?*

— WHERE: HELP/HINDER —

Purpose: To achieve flexibility in defining a space with or in spite of another player.

Focus: On helping, then hindering contacts other players make with objects in the *Where*.

Description: Two players. *Where, Who,* and *What* agreed upon. Using a detailed floor plan, players make contact with every object in the *Where* while maintaining relationship and activity. When coached **Help!**, players help one another make contact. When coached **Hinder!**, players throw up obstacles to one another to prevent the other contacting the objects. Helping or hindering must be appropriate to the scene.

Notes: 1. See Note 1 above (WHERE WITH OBSTACLES). Tension between players is not necessary for these games.

2. Ask for a great deal of detail in the floor plans.

3. The game is over when both players have made contact with everything in the *Where*. However, it may be necessary to call **One minute!** to heighten the playing and help the playing come to an end.

Help each other make contact with the objects!
Now keep each other from contacting the objects!
Work on the problem!
Help!
Hinder!
Help!
Hinder!
Make contacts make sense!
Integrate obstacles!
Have a reason for setting up obstacles!
Avoid dialogue!

Did players contact the objects through who they were and what they were doing, or was it random contact simply to touch the objects?
When did the Where *appear?*
Players, do you agree?

— THE SPECIALIZED WHERE —

Purpose: To make the invisible setting visible.

Focus: On showing *Where* through the use of physical objects.

Description: Two or more players on a team. All teams are given the same general *Where* (a hotel room, an office, a schoolroom, etc.). Each team, in its own way, is to specialize the general *Where* (a hotel room *in Paris*, a *hospital* office, a *jungle* schoolroom) and choose *Who* and *What*.

Note: Encourage players to specialize the *Where* by making unusual choices (an office in a space satellite, a jungle hotel room).

Show! Don't tell!
Explore! Heighten!
Heighten the specific objects!
Help each other!

Did players choose distinctive objects that brought their specialized Where *to life?*
Or did they have to tell us where they were through talking?
Players, do you agree?

— WHERE GAME (SCENE) ———————————

Purpose: To test whether the players have succeeded in physicalizing the setting, making the invisible visible.

Focus: On showing an audience *Where, Who,* and *What* through the use of and/or contact with all objects in the *Where.*

Description: Count off for teams of two to four players. Each team agrees on *Where, Who,* and *What* and sketches a floor plan of *Where* on paper. As *Where, Who,* and *What* are played out, each player (referring to the floor plan) must make contact with every object in the floor plan. Players place actual chairs needed in the playing area, tack the floor plan up for easy referral, and call curtain when ready. They then perform an improvised scene.

Example: *Where* = kitchen, *Who* = family members, *What* = eating breakfast. Floor plan includes refrigerator, cupboards, table, sink, etc.

Notes: 1. Always check what audience saw against the actual floor plan.

2. Coach players to avoid planning how to use each object, as pre-planning takes all spontaneity out of the playing.

3. Players shouldn't be frustrated by the absence of physical objects on the stage. In many theater traditions (those of Sophocles or Shakespeare, for example) actors worked on a bare stage with only hand props, dialogue, and their actions to indicate setting.

Share with the audience!
Show! Don't tell!
Each player must contact every object on the floor plan!
Keep objects in space and out of your head!
Look at your floor plan!

Did players use all objects on the floor plan?
Audience, what objects did players show us?
Players, check them off against the actual floor plan.
Did players show Where, Who, *and* What?
Or did they tell?
Were objects in space or in players' heads?
Did the players use imaginary objects or were they made in real space?
Players, did you walk through tables?

— INVOLVEMENT WITH THE — IMMEDIATE ENVIRONMENT

Purpose: To integrate conversation (dialogue) with the establishment of a setting.

Focus: On showing *Where,* while talking, by making repeated contact with space objects in the immediate environment.

Description: Teams of two or more players, preferably seated, agree on *Where* and *Who* they are. *While involved in a discussion,* players show where they are by continuous involvement with small space objects within arm's reach.

Examples: 1. Two players waiting for a bus find chipped paint on the bench, fallen leaves, specks of dirt, etc.

2. Two magicians demonstrate their skills.

3. A short-order cook approaches lunch hour while arguing with a waitress.

Note: Caution players not to perform a full activity such as eating a meal, but to be *occupied* with a conversation and *pre-occupied* with the focus. When both occur simultaneously, extraordinary life and detail are apparent in the scene.

Keep focus on the objects you find around you!
Show us who you are through the immediate environment!
Let the objects reveal themselves!

Did where players were come to life through the objects?
Did players show us or tell us? Who were they?
Did dialogue stop when objects were being handled?
Did the objects reveal themselves or were they invented by players?

Who Games

Ideas and terms important to this section:

Memories: They are cerebral and historical. If relied upon solely in building a character, they limit full-body response to a new event.

Experience: A living process which cannot be reconstructed through memory.

— NEW YORK (LEMONADE)★ ——————

Purpose: To make players aware of the possibilities of nonverbal communication.

Description: The players divide into two equal teams and stand on parallel goals twenty or more feet apart. First team decides on a trade, an occupation, to be acted out and then advances toward the other team while the following dialogue takes place:

> First team: Here we come.
> Second team: Where from?
> First team: New York.
> Second team: What's your trade?
> First team: Lemonade.
> Second team: Give us some.

The first team's players come as near to the second as they dare and act out their trade, or occupation, each in his or her own way. The second team tries to identify what is being acted out; and when one player identifies the trade correctly, the first team runs for its home base, while the second team tries to tag them. All who are tagged have been captured and join the taggers' side. Second team chooses a trade and the dialogue is repeated, followed by the acting, as before. Both sides have the same number of turns, and the one having the largest number of players at the end wins.

Notes: 1. This game can be played more easily indoors if, instead of running toward a goal, the first team squats when the trade is guessed. If a player is tagged before he or she can squat, a capture has been made.

2. Variations of this game can be played by acting out animals, flowers, trees, and other objects instead of trades.

— How Old Am I? —

Purpose: To establish early orientation to character.

Focus: On showing a chosen age.

Description: Establish a simple setting, such as a corner bus stop, with a bench in the playing area. Each player focuses on his or her chosen age. If time is short, five or six players may be at the bus stop at the same time. However, players are not to interact in any way.

Notes: 1. Players will tend to act out their old frames of reference, which is expected within this game.

2. Many will rely on character qualities and role-playing.

3. We all have stowed away countless characters. Repeating the age sends a signal into this vast storehouse, and by letting the focus work for us it delivers us a character quality fitting for our bodies. Hidden memory systems are called upon. Allow data to emerge.

4. This game, of course, is of great value in helping young people understand the problems and needs of the elderly.

Feel your age!
Feel the age in your feet!
Your eyes!
The bus is a block away!
It's coming closer!
It's here!
(If you wish player to explore further possibilities):
It's held up in traffic!

How old was this player?
Player, do you agree with audience players?
Was the age in your head?
Or in the body?
Does age sixty-five feel the same way to everybody?
Does a person who has taken care to stay healthy move the same way as a person the same age who has been careless?

—— WHAT DO I DO FOR A LIVING? ——

Purpose: To show the availability of hidden resources.

Focus: On the chosen occupation.

Description: Establish a simple *Where,* such as a bus stop. Teams of five or more. Each player chooses an occupation, writes it on a slip of paper, and hands it to the teacher. Player enters the playing area and waits, focused on occupation. Players do not know one another and avoid dialogue.

Notes: 1. The evaluation should provoke insights into physicalizing character. It should be most casual. Later games will allow other insights into character.

2. Jokes, "acting," and clowning are evidence of a resistance to the focus.

3. Allow several minutes for the effects of the focus to become manifest.

Variation: Mix up the occupations and pass them out at random to players just prior to entering the playing area.

Feel the occupation in your whole body!
Hands! Feet! Neck!
(When occupations begin to emerge):
Keep repeating your profession!
The bus is coming!

What were the occupations?
Did players show or tell?
Players, do you agree?
Is it only through activity that we can show what we do for a living?
Players, explain to audience how you knew what your character acted like.
Do you know anybody like the character you were playing?

WHO AM I?

Purpose: To build a character through showing, not telling.

Focus: On involvement in the immediate activity until the *Who* is revealed.

Description: Whole group or large teams. One player volunteers to leave the room while the group decides who player will be, for example: union leader, cook in the Vatican, circus barker, etc. — ideally someone who is usually surrounded by much activity or institutional life. Then the first player is asked to return and sit in the playing area, while the others, one at a time or in small groups, enter in relation to the *Who* and become involved in appropriate activity until the *Who* is known.

Notes: 1. The most difficult part of WHO AM I? is to keep the unknowing player from making it a guessing game and the others from supplying clues. *Who* will emerge if player remains open (in waiting) to what is happening and involved in the immediate activity.

    2. Choosing famous people should be avoided until the group is familiar with the exercise.

    3. The exercise reaches its natural ending when the unknowing player shows by word or deed that *Who* has surfaced. Players may, however, continue the scene when *Who* is known.

    4. After the focus is clearly understood, WHO AM I? can be used in the regular curriculum study of historical personages, scientists, engineers, inventors, authors, etc. Focusing on the immediate environment (*Where*) will bring greater dimension and understanding of the chosen subject.

Don't try to guess who you are!
Wait until you know!
Be part of what is happening!
Ask no questions!
Who you are will become clear!
Other players, give no clues!
Show! Don't tell!
Don't give it away!
No hurry! Wait!

Did the player try to guess the Who *or did he or she wait until what was happening made it clear? Player, do you agree?*

— WHO GAME

Purpose: To show, not tell, character.

Focus: On communicating, through relationship and setting, the identity of a character.

Description: Two players, A and B. A is seated in the playing area. B enters. B has a predetermined character relationship with A, but has not told A what it is. By the way B relates to A, A discovers who A is.

Notes: 1. The game ends as soon as A realizes *Who.* But, if time allows, continue if there is involvement between the players.

2. After evaluation, reverse positions and let A choose a relationship with B.

3. If players tell instead of show, have players use gibberish. (See Gibberish series.)

4. Once the game is learned it can be correlated with social studies or reading assignments.

5. The "recognition scene" is an ancient dramatic convention in which long-lost family members discover their true identities and are reunited. There are many examples of this in Greek tragedy. And there are hilarious parodies of the scene in *Cox and Box*, Wilde's *The Importance of Being Ernest*, Ionesco's *The Bald Soprano*, and Beckett's *Waiting for Godot.*

*Show **Where!***
No questions!
Wait! No hurry!
Let who you are become clear!

Did B show the relationship or tell!
*Did A wait to allow **Who** to become clear!*

— KNOCKING ★ —————————————————

Purpose: To develop acuteness in hearing.

Focus: On identifying an object by listening.

Description: All players close eyes while leader knocks distinctly three times on any object in the room and then walks noiselessly away from it. Leader tells players when to open eyes and calls on one to name the object knocked on. Should that player fail, another is chosen. Should all show confusion, leader asks players to close eyes again and repeats the knocking.

Notes: 1. This game is a traditional children's game used here as a warm-up to WHO'S KNOCKING? FEELING SELF WITH SELF and SENDING HEARING OUT are also excellent lead-ins to that game.

    2. Should children peek, remind all that this is a hearing game.

    3. More advanced students may be interested in discussing how they know the direction from which a sound comes. How do stereophonic record players work?

How do you know what is being knocked on?
Does wood sound different from metal?
Does a wall sound different from a desk?
Why?

—— WHO'S KNOCKING? ————————————

Purpose: To develop nonverbal communication.

Focus: On showing the *Who, Where,* and *What* through knocking.

Description: One player remains out of sight of the audience and knocks on a door. This player is to communicate who is knocking, for what reason, where, time of day, weather, etc., by the way he or she knocks. Some examples might include a policeman at night, a rejected suitor at a sweetheart's door, a messenger from the king, a very young child in a closet.

Notes: 1. In evaluation, the teacher will find that many observers did not know the exact circumstances, the *Where, Who,* and *What,* of a knock. Now that all know, have player repeat the knocking. Observers will listen more intently and find communication clearer now, when they do not have to guess.

2. Repeating the knock after evaluation keeps audience players part of the game and involved in what other players are doing.

3. Some questions in evaluation may be unanswerable, but asking them may bring new insights to the players.

4. A knock at the door actually has no intrinsic meaning. It is a useful social-studies exercise to have students imagine a wide variety of situations, settings, and historical periods in which a knock at the door might mean very different things. (Examples: an apartment in a totalitarian country, a college dormitory room, a doctor's office closed for the night.)

Share your knock!
Try it again!
Heighten it!

Who is knocking? At what door?
What time of day?
For what purpose?

— Showing Who through ——————
Use of an Object

Purpose: To define character in terms of tools and posses-
sions.

Focus: On showing *Who* through the use of an object.

Description: Two players agree upon an object that will
show who they are. They use that object within an activity.

Example: *Who:* a teacher and student; the object: a
chalkboard. A writes a math problem with an incorrect
solution on the board. B shakes head, erases the solution,
and writes another. A says, "I see!"

Note: Players are not to pre-plan *Where*, *Who*, and *What*
beyond choosing *Who* and the object, but are to keep focus
on the problem and let it help them.

Show!
Don't tell!
Make the object real!

Audience, who are they?
Did they show us or tell us?

—— CHANGING EMOTION ———————

Purpose: To physicalize emotion.

Focus: On showing emotions or feelings through use of space objects.

Description: Single player completes an activity with focus on showing a definite feeling through use and handling of objects. Then the activity must be reversed, and player proceeds to undo what has been done, showing the changed feeling through the same handling and use.

Examples: A girl dresses for a dance, showing pleasure or apprehension by the way she takes her dress from a closet. After learning the dance is canceled, she shows disappointment or relief by putting the dress back in the closet. A boy gets permission to drive his father's car. The car won't start.

Notes: 1. At the turning point, the director can ring the phone or send another player to provide the necessary information.

2. If changing emotion or feeling is shown only through facial mannerisms, players are "acting" and have not understood the meaning of physicalization. Using props and body is essential.

3. If students are studying particular historical or literary characters it may be valuable to have them try this game while playing roles. How might President Washington or Tom Sawyer or Sally Ride respond to a disappointment?

Show that thought by doing!
Explore that object!

Was the activity identical before and after the turning point?
Was the feeling communicated through body changes?
What does pleasure do to one physically?
How does disappointment affect movement?

What Games

– WHAT AM I EATING? TASTING? ———— SMELLING? HEARING? ★

Purpose: To define an object or substance without using words.

Focus: On communicating information through action; on showing, not telling.

Description: The group is divided into two equal teams. Each team secretly decides on something to eat (or drink, taste, smell, hear, feel, look at, etc.). Then a game of NEW YORK is played with players communicating not a trade but whatever it is they are eating, tasting, etc. If a game of tag is not possible, the first team up stands in front of the audience and each onstage player, in his or her own way, communicates what is being eaten, drunk, heard, etc. Rather than call out guesses until the players start to run away, audience players huddle together and come to group agreement as to what is being communicated. The teacher may make this a scoring game.

Notes: 1. There should be no dialogue among players. Although they stand together, each player works alone.

2. Even without dialogue, players can *tell* by using sign language—making obvious physical movements. This is, of course, to be discouraged. Players *show* when they are focused on what is to be communicated.

3. Stress that when focus is complete, audience players can *see* what is being eaten, drunk, smelled, etc.

Show!
Don't tell!
Communicate!
Audience: Be open for the communication!
Show, don't tell!

Did players show or tell?
Players, do you agree with audience players?

—— HERE WE GO ROUND —————— THE MULBERRY BUSH ★

Description: The players join hands in a ring and skip 'round, singing the song. "Here we go round the mulberry bush,/The mulberry bush, the mulberry bush;/Here we go round the mulberry bush,/On a cold and frosty morning." Then they agree what kind of work they want to do and, standing in place, play the activity decided upon. (Traditionally these activities centered on getting dressed and housework.) For instance, if washing the face is chosen, each vigorously washes his or her face while singing: "This is the way we wash our face,/Wash our face, wash our face;/This is the way we wash our face,/On a cold and frosty morning." On the words "On a cold and frosty morning" all shiver and, pretending to wrap shawls or scarves closely around their shoulders, turn completely around.

Repeat "Here we go round the mulberry bush," as in the beginning. The players then suggest various activities, such as combing hair, shining shoes, mending clothes, etc.; and when they are completely dressed, they sing, "This is the way we go to school," skipping gaily in a circle. The verse "Here we go round the mulberry bush," etc., is sung between all but the last two verses.

Notes: 1. As the players become familiar with the game, the verses are sung without stopping; the leader simply pauses on "This is the way" until a player suggests the activity, then all take it up and the game continues.

2. This is an English version of the song. Probably the most familiar version in America is printed in the right column.

Here we go round the mulberry bush,
The mulberry bush, the mulberry bush;
Here we go round the mulberry bush,
So early in the morning.

This is the way we wash our clothes,
Wash our clothes, wash our clothes;
This is the way we wash our clothes,
So early Monday morning.
Here we go round the mulberry bush etc.

This is the way we iron our clothes etc.,
So early Tuesday morning.
Here we go round the mulberry bush etc.

This is the way we scrub the floors etc.,
So early Wednesday morning.
Here we go round the mulberry bush etc.

Here we go round the mul-ber-ry bush the mul-berry bush the mul-ber-ry bush;

Here we go round the mul-ber-ry bush on a cold and frost-y morn-ing

—IDENTIFYING OBJECTS ★ ——————

Purpose: To develop player's sense of the attributes of objects.

Focus: To identify an object through touch alone.

Description: Players stand in a circle. One player is called to the center and stands with a hand behind the back. After first showing it to the class, the teacher places some actual object in the player's hand. Using only the sense of touch, the player is to identify the object. When the player identifies the object, he or she may look at it. Then another player is called to the center and is given a new object to identify.

Notes: 1. Ask the sidecoaching questions only if the player is at a loss to identify the object.

2. Choose objects that are recognizable although not used every day (tiddlywink, postage stamp, playing card, paper of pins, pencil sharpener, rubber stamp, apple, etc.).

What is it for?
Is it warm or cool?
What is it made of?

— INVOLVEMENT WITH LARGE OBJECTS ——

Purpose: To create an action through use of space objects in an environment.

Focus: On physical involvement with a large object in the space.

Description: Single player, or large group of players all working individually. Each player selects and becomes involved with a large entangling object. Examples include: a spider web, a boa constrictor, forest vines, a collapsed parachute, etc.

Notes: 1. Be certain the player's focus is on the *object* and *not* on emotional responses to the involvement. This is an important difference and one that comes up continuously throughout the work.

2. The same rule (as in Note 1) is true in stage combat: players must focus on the object rather than their emotional response to danger. Battle scenes on stage are rehearsed by choreographers who make actors concentrate on the weapons rather than on their feelings. This focus makes a fight more believable and less dangerous to performers.

Give life to the object!
Use your whole body!
Allow the object its place in space!
Explore the object!
Show!
Don't tell!

Was focus complete or incomplete?
Did players show us the object or tell us?
Was the object in the players' heads or in the space?
Players, do you agree?

— INVOLVEMENT WITHOUT HANDS ——

Purpose: To work together creating an action despite restrictions.

Focus: On showing and manipulating an agreed upon object without using hands.

Description: Two or more players. Players agree between themselves on an animate or inanimate object. Players are to set object between them in motion without using their hands.

Examples: Pushing a rock, pushing a car, getting a toboggan to move, mountain climbing (rope tied to waist), raising a board to shoulder.

Notes: 1. Do not let the players take an obviously no-hands task such as mashing grapes with the feet, for this is resistance to the focus.

2. Watch for spontaneity and unusual ways of putting the objects in motion.

3. As a first step to the above exercise try something that ties all the players together such as a chain gang.

Work together!
No hands!
Use your full body!
Shoulders!
Knees!
Elbows!
Neck!
Back!
Get the object moving!

Did they show us the object or tell us about it?

——WHAT'S BEYOND: ACTIVITY——————

Purpose: To develop nonverbal communication.

Focus: On communicating activity that has just taken place offstage.

Description: A player enters, walks through the playing area, and exits. Without speech or unnecessary activity, the player communicates what activity he or she was involved in just before entering the playing area. After the audience guesses the activity, another player enters, communicating another activity.

Variation: Instead of communicating what has just happened before entering, the player communicates what is about to happen after exiting.

Notes: 1. Keep evaluation on the focus only. The only thing of interest is what has just happened or is about to happen.

2. If this exercise is given early, players should keep what happened simple (e.g., shoveling snow outside).

3. When repeated later, the activity could be based on a relationship, such as a quarrel with a friend, a wedding, a job interview, bad news.

4. See note on showing, not telling, in introduction to Chapter 13.

Show! Don't tell!
Let your body reflect what
just took place!
Heighten it!

Variation:
Show! Don't tell!
Let your body reflect
what activity will follow!

What had just happened?
Did player show or tell?
What will happen?
Did player show or tell?

Chapter 10:
COMMUNICATING WITH WORDS

Most theater games require dialogue. But fear of verbal exchange can be very great.

During some of the earlier games, when children are becoming part of an action (as in PART OF A WHOLE, ACTIVITY), some players may silently mouth words, in which case it's a good idea to sidecoach **Share your voice!** Players may even ask, "Should we talk?" Quietly encourage them to do so if they wish.

Gibberish games take the voice to another level of communication.[1] The following games focus on the word.

In order to avoid the stilted dialogue of inexperienced players, the dialogue part of the games is linked with at least one other strong focus. When there are multiple stimuli, the tension/energy needed to solve the problem is created.[2] Players are so caught up in the effort to keep focus that dialogue flows naturally without the painfully forced quality of a player trying to be funny, smart, sad, or whatever. In time players learn to trust that, when they are on focus, the words they need will appear. They don't have to think about them. In games as in everyday life, words can be used to say what the listener wants to hear and to conceal what the listener needs to know.

□ *When keeping focus in a game, a player hasn't time to worry about approval or disapproval.*

Further development of skills taught in this chapter:

Will be found in Chapters 14, 15, and 16 on media, scenebuilding, and Story Theater.

[1]See Chapter 11: Communicating with Sounds.

[2]See Chapter 12: Multiple-Stimulus Games.

—— HANDWRITING LARGE ——————

Purpose: To discover the power in an individual word or phrase.

Focus: On writing words as large as possible.

Description: Using the chalkboard, each player, one by one, tries to fill the chalkboard with a favorite word or phrase.

Note: Do not be concerned with spelling or penmanship for this exercise. Those players who focus most intently on a word or phrase are most likely to misspell or distort it. Players are asked only to fill as large a space as possible with a word or phrase.

Use your whole body to fill the board!
Write the word as large as you possibly can!
Fill the whole space with your word!
Feel the word!

Did the player fill the space?
Or could player have used even more of the chalkboard?

—— HANDWRITING SMALL ——————

Purpose: To discover the independent existence of a word or phrase.

Focus: On writing words or phrases as small as possible.

Description: Full group working individually at desks, each player with a piece of paper and a very sharp pencil. Holding the hand in no motion, players think and write favorite words, phrases, and sentences as small as possible.

Notes: 1. NO MOTION is an ideal warm-up for this game.

2. Again, do not be concerned with proper spelling or handwriting style. Players simply try to write words as small as possible.

3. Students have a great deal of fun with this exercise. Try it for a few minutes now and then. If students become frustrated, drop the exercise immediately!

4. This exercise follows the same principle as swinging a pendulum (a ball on a string) without any overt movement. Once the player *thinks* movement even though he or she tries to hold the hand still, the ball begins to move back and forth and around.

Write small!
Small!
Very tiny!
Let your body do the work!
Hold the hand still and see what you get!
Think the words and sentences you are writing!

Players pass papers.
Can the words, written very, very small, be read by another?

— HANDWRITING BLINDFOLDED ——————

Purpose: To gain new familiarity with a word or phrase.

Focus: On writing words or phrases without looking.

Description: Players in full group at desks, or one by one at the chalkboard, close eyes and write words or phrases without looking. Using a blindfold makes the game more amusing.

Note: Spelling and writing style are not as important as the ability of other players to read the words or phrases.

Write normally!
Cross your t's!
Dot your i's!
When you are finished, look and see what you have written!
Once again!
Let your eyes stay closed and let your hand write the words!
Cross t's and dot i's!

Did players cross all t's and dot all i's?
Can you read each other's words and phrases?
Player, can you read your own words and phrases?

— DUMB CRAMBO ★ ——————

Focus: On dramatizing a word.

Description: The players are divided in two groups, one of which goes out of the room while the other chooses a verb that can be dramatized. The outside group is called back and given a word which rhymes with the verb that has been chosen. After consulting among themselves, the members of the group that was sent from the room act out the verb they think is the correct one. If it proves to be such, the other group applauds; if not, they shake their heads. The guessing group continues to act out verbs until the correct one is discovered, whereupon this group chooses a verb for the other one to act. Should a group be forced to give up, that group must continue to act a new word chosen by the other group.

Variation: A single player may also be sent out of the room while the group chooses a verb. The player then returns and, after being told a word which rhymes with the verb chosen, acts out verbs until he or she gets the correct one.

— NAME SIX ★ ——————————————————

Purpose: To help students communicate quickly and easily using words.

Focus: On quickly naming six objects with the same beginning letter.

Description: All the players except one, who stands in the center, sit in a circle. The center player closes eyes while the others pass any small object from one to the other. When the center player claps hands, the player who is caught with the object in hand must keep it until the center player points at him or her and names a letter of the alphabet. (No effort is made to hide the object from the center player.) Then the player who has the object must start it on its way immediately so that it passes through the hands of each of the players in the circle in turn. By the time it returns, the player must have named six objects, each beginning with the letter chosen. If the player does not succeed in naming six objects in the time that it takes for the object to make the round of the circle, that player must change places with the one in the center. If the circle is small, the object should be passed around two or more times.

Notes: 1. This traditional game is useful as a warm-up to quiet a group.

2. It can easily be adapted for curriculum needs when coordinated with any memorization students may be doing: name six numbers divisible by four, six parts of the body, six of the fifty states (or of the original colonies), six verbs, etc. This game sometimes works best if the teacher takes the center position.

3. For children too young to know all letter/sound correspondences, have the center player call out a word and the player with the object say six other words that begin with the same sound.

4. Another variation for young players is for the center player to call out a category (such as "animals" or "fruit" or "things with wheels"). Then six things that belong in that category must be named.

— Singing Syllables ★ ————————————

Purpose: To give players a new sense of the spoken word.

Focus (For "It"): To "sense" the word in the song.

Description: Players sit in a circle. One goes from the room and the others choose a word — for example, "Washington." The syllables of the word are distributed around the circle — "Wash" is given to the first group of players, "ing" to the second group, and "ton" to the third group so that all groups have an assigned syllable. To a familiar tune (such as "Yankee Doodle" or "Dixie") players sing their group's syllable over and over. The odd player ("It") walks about from group to group and tries to piece the word together, using as many guesses as needed. The game may be made more difficult by having players change places after the syllables have been given out, thus dispersing the groups. All groups sing their syllables to the same tune simultaneously.

— Kitty Wants a Corner ★ ————————————

Purpose: To produce off-balance moments. Players must interact.

Focus: To avoid becoming — to stop being — "It."

Description: Full group stands around the perimeter of the playing space, except for one player (the kitty), who stands in the middle. The spot where each person stands is "a corner." Player who is "It" approaches another player and says, "Kitty wants a corner!" The reply to this is "See my next-door neighbor." Kitty continues this dialogue with fellow players in turn, while trying to jump into a corner vacated by other players, whose business it is to trade places without kitty pouncing upon a corner. The odd player out, in such a case, is "It."

── Isabella ★ ──────────────────────────

Description: The children join hands in a ring. One child, representing Isabella, stands in the center of the ring. The children walk in a circle singing:

1. Isabella, Isabella, Isabella, farewell.
   Last night when we parted, I left you broken hearted,
   And on a green mountain you were standing alone.

   All stand and sing

2. Choose your sweetheart, choose your sweetheart,
   Choose your sweetheart, farewell.

   Isabella chooses one of the children; the ring is left open where the chosen child stood, and through this opening Isabella and her partner walk hand in hand a short distance away, while the children in the ring continue singing.

3. Go to church, love, go to church, love,
   Go to church, love, farewell.

   Isabella and her partner kneel.

4. Kneel down, love, kneel down, love,
   Kneel down, love, farewell.

5. Put the ring on, put the ring on,
   Put the ring on, farewell.

   Isabella pretends to put ring on her partner's finger.

6. Come back, love, come back, love,
   Come back, love, farewell.

   Isabella and her partner re-enter the ring where they went out.

7. What's for dinner, love? what's for dinner, love?
   What's for dinner, love? farewell.

   Children close the ring and walk to the left. Isabella and her partner stand with both hands joined.

8. Roast beef and plum pudding, roast beef and plum pudding,
   Roast beef and plum pudding for dinner today.

   The circle skips rapidly to the left, while Isabella and her partner with both hands joined skip rapidly round and round in place in the center.
   Isabella and her partner then bow to each other and Isabella joins the ring. The game is repeated with her partner as Isabella.

Viola Spolin

Is - a - bel - la, Is - a - bel - la, Is - a - bel - la, fare - well. Last night when we part - ed, I

left you bro - ken - heart - ed, And on a green moun - tain, you were standing a - lone. Choose your

Last verse.

sweet-heart choose your sweet-heart; Choose your sweet-heart, fare - well. Go to

Church, love, go to church, love, go to church, love, fare - well. Kneel well. Roast beef and plum

pud - ding, roast beef and plum pud - ding, Roast beef and plum pud - ding for din - ner to - day

PRINCESS THORN ROSA ★

Description: Familiarize group with melody and first verse. (The rest of the lyrics will come with playing.) Players are chosen to be Thorn Rosa, the witch, and the prince. A small group of players joins hands to form the castle around Thorn Rosa in the center, and the remaining players join hands around the castle to form the thorny hedge.

Witch and prince are outside the hedge on opposite sides and a little distance away.

Verse 1: Inner circle (castle) walks to right; outer circle (thorny hedge) walks left.

Verse 2: Both circles stand still; inner circle raises arms to form the castle.

Verse 3: Circles stand as for Verse 2. Ugly witch comes into castle, touches Thorn Rosa (who falls asleep), and immediately goes away. Witch may join the outer circle if desired.

Verses 4 and 5: Circles stand.

Verse 6: Prince cuts down the thorny hedge with his sword. Joined hands drop in appropriate places.

Verse 7: Prince enters castle and touches Thorn Rosa who wakes at his touch.

Verses 8 and 9: Thorn Rosa and the prince join hands and, pulling against one another, they skip round and round in place in the center. The inner circle dances gaily to the right and the outer to the left. Tempo is increased for Verse 9.

Notes: 1. This traditional singing game is a variation of the classic story of Sleeping Beauty and appears in *Folk Games of Denmark and Sweden* by Dagny Pederson and Neva L. Boyd (Chicago: H.T. FitzSimons Co., Inc.).

2. This game has often been used as a performance piece. The story can be expanded on and dialogue added. (See STORYTELLING and BUILDING A STORY.)

1. Thorn Rosa was a pretty child, pretty child, pretty child. Thorn Rosa was a pretty child, pretty child.
2. She lived up in a castle high, etc.
3. One day there came an ugly witch, etc.
4. Thorn Rosa slept a hundred years, etc.
5. A thorny hedge grew giant high, etc.
6. One day there came a handsome prince, etc.
7. Thorn Rosa wakened at his touch, etc.
8. Oh, all our hearts are happy now, etc.
9. Tra la la, la la, la la la, etc.

Thorn Ro-sa was a pret-ty child, pret-ty child pret-ty child. Thorn Ro-sa was a pret-ty child pret-ty child

GIVE & TAKE WARM-UP ★ ——————————

Purpose: To help players connect with one another.

Focus: On seeing and hearing.

Description: Players stand in a circle. Any player may start a movement. If any player is moving all other players must hold (no movement). Any player can make a motion at any time but must hold if another player starts a motion. Sounds may be considered movements. Players sensing another player moving (giving) are said to be "taking."

Notes: 1. "Hold" is used instead of "freeze." "Freeze" is total stoppage; "hold" is waiting to move as soon as one may do so.

2. For younger children, begin by having each child stick with one movement.

Hold your movement!
Continue the flow of your movement!
Hold when another player moves!
Give!

— GIVE & TAKE

Purpose: To be in a state of nonverbal agreement with partner, while in readiness to act with the other team.

Focus: On listening/hearing with partner to know when to give and take.

Description: (Two tables, each with two chairs, are useful for this exercise.) Players count off into teams of four. Teams subdivide into teams of two. Each subteam (sitting at its own table) pursues a separate conversation. While continuing separate conversations, both subteams must hear the other subteam so as to know when to give or take.

Part 1: Teacher calls **Table 1!** and **Table 2!** until how to play becomes clear to both subteams. Both subteams begin conversing at the same time. When table 1 is called, subteam 2 must fade out (submerge action) and give focus to subteam 1. When table 2 is called, subteam 1 fades. Players must understand that a fade-out is not a freeze. Players at table out of focus hold action, relationship, and conversation silently in no motion but stay prepared to continue actively when it is time to take focus once more.

Part 2: When mutual giving of focus to opposite subteam is understood, players are asked to continue their conversations, giving focus back and forth without being sidecoached.

Part 3: Continuing as above, both subteams try to *take* the focus from the other. The subteam which *holds* the attention of the audience has taken the focus.

Part 4: Both subteams give and take the focus without sidecoaching.

Notes: 1. Players on subteams learn to give and take as *one* unit. This develops receiving and sending abilities on a nonverbal level.

2. Use **Give and take!** as sidecoaching in any game whenever players all move and talk at the same time without hearing one another. It will help players discover the focus of a scene.

3. See following game for an application of **Give and take!** to another game.

Part 1:
Table 1! Table 2 fade!
Keep relationship within the fade!
Do not freeze!
Sit relaxed in no motion!
Table 2! Table 1 fade!

Part 2:
Give! Play the game!
Play as one unit!

Part 3:
Take! Take! (Until focus is taken. Audience will know when focus is taken.)

Part 4:
You are on your own!
Give and take!
Know when to give!
Know when to take!
Play the game!

Subteam 1, did you have trouble knowing when your partner wanted to give?
Audience, could you tell when one member of a subteam didn't want to give and the other did?
Players, did you take the focus in Part 4 before the other team had given it?
Other subteam, do you agree?
Audience, do you agree?

— Give & Take for Reading —————————

Purpose: To help players pay full attention to one another.

Focus: On trying to take the opportunity to read aloud.

Description: Players divide into teams evenly matched in reading skills. Simultaneously reading the same passage silently, all players in a group *give* the opportunity to read aloud to any player who *takes* it (starts to read aloud). Only one player at a time can read aloud. A player may take, from another player, the opportunity to read aloud whenever he or she wants. Frequent give and take is desirable. Skipping words or repeating the last words of the previous reader is not allowed.

Note: With all players giving and taking and some players catching other players even in mid-word or phrase, this exercise adds excitement to reading aloud.

(Only as needed):
Give when someone takes!
Take when someone gives!
Stay with the exact words being read aloud!
Only one player reads at once!
Share your voice!

Did the reading aloud become one flowing piece as though just one person were reading?
Or did it stop and start and repeat itself?

— Seeing the Word —————————

Purpose: To stimulate fuller sense perceptions.

Focus: On the event being narrated.

Description: Single player. Player goes on stage and describes an actual experience, such as taking a trip, watching a football game, or visiting someone. The player maintains the focus (on the event) all during the sidecoaching. It is very important to continue narrating while receiving the coaching.

Note: As greater perception is awakened by sidecoaching, note at what moment player begins to leave the *word* and relate to the *scene.* The speaking voice will become natural, the body will relax, and words will flow. When a player is no longer depending on words but is focused on the environment that was entered, then all artificiality and stilted speech disappear. A past event has become a present-time experience.

Focus on the color!
The sounds! Weather!
People! Smells!
See yourself!

Did this scene feel real?
Were you hand in hand with the storyteller on the trip?

── Mirror Speech ──────────────

Purpose: To follow the follower verbally, creating dialogue.

Focus: On mirroring/reflecting another player's words *out loud.*

Description: Teams of two players. Players face each other and choose a subject of conversation. One player is the initiator and starts the conversation. The other player is the reflector and mirrors *out loud* the words of the initiator (for a discussion of these terms see Chapter 8). Both players will be speaking the same words out loud at the exact same moment. When ***Change!*** is called, roles are reversed. The reflector becomes the initiator of speech and the old initiator becomes the new reflector. Changeovers must be made with *no stop* in the flow of words. After a time, no more changes will be called by the director. Players will "follow the follower" in speech, thinking and saying the same words simultaneously and without conscious effort.

Notes: 1. Initiators should be coached to avoid asking questions. If a question is asked, the reflector must *reflect* the question, not *answer* the question.

2. The difference between repeating the words of the other and reflecting the words of the other must be felt with the whole body (the senses) before "follow the follower" can take place. When true reflection takes place, the time lapse between initiator and reflector becomes very short, near nothing. In a sense, players connect with one another on the same word and become one mind, open to one another.

3. If time is limited, have group count off into teams of three players, one of which is the sidecoach. All teams play the game at the same time in different areas of the room.

4. This game can also be played having players reflect one another's speech silently. See FOLLOW THE FOLLOWER.

Reflector, stay on the same word!
Reflect what you hear!
Reflect the question! Don't answer it!
Share your voice!
Change the reflector!
Keep the flow of words between you!
Stay on the same word!
Change! Change!
(When players are speaking as one voice, without time lag):
You are on your own!
Don't initiate!
Follow the initiator!
Follow the follower!

Audience players, did onstage players stay on the same word at the same time?
Players, did you know when you initiated speech and when you reflected speech?
Did you know when you were following the follower?
All players, what is the difference between repeating speech and reflecting speech?

— VERBALIZING THE WHERE, PART 1 ————

Purpose: To make players more aware of their environment.

Focus: On remaining in the *Where,* while verbalizing every involvement, observation, relation, etc. in it.

Description: Teams of two players agree on *Where, Who,* and *What* and sit in playing area. Without leaving their chairs, players improvise an event (scene) verbally, describing their actions in the *Where,* and their relation to the other players. When dialogue is necessary, it is spoken directly to the other player, interrupting the narration. All verbalization is in the present tense.

Example: Player 1: "I tie my red-and-white apron around my waist and reach for the cloth-covered cookbook on the table. I sit down at the table and open the book, looking for a recipe. . . ."

Player 2: "I open the screen door and run into the kitchen. Darn it, I let the door slam again! 'Hey, Mom, I'm hungry. What's for dinner?'"

Notes: 1. This exercise can aid in breaking players of opinions and attitudes in their work.

2. Do not go on to the next game unless players have understood the focus, and it has worked for them.

3. So-called observing is usually filled with personal attitudes—seeing something through dos and don'ts, prejudices, assumptions, etc.—the very opposite of simply seeing what is at hand. Just seeing, right now, allows players, whether writing or speaking, to open as-yet-closed doors within themselves.

4. RELATING AN INCIDENT ADDING COLOR, Chapter 15, is an excellent warm-up for this game and the one following.

Keep it in the present time!
Describe the objects that show **Where!**
Describe other players for us!
Keep opinions out!
See yourself in action!
Use dialogue when it seems right!
Tell us how your hands feel on the chair!
No opinions!
That's an attitude!
An assumption!

Did player stay in the Where?
Was the player in the head (giving background information, judgments, opinions, attitudes)?
Players, do you agree?
Was there more that could have been said?
Might the story have taken another direction?
How should it have ended?
What other characters would you like to have seen?
How would you have changed the Where?

—— Verbalizing the Where, Part 2——

Purpose: To make the invisible visible.

Focus: On retaining physical reality from Verbalizing the Where, Part 1.

Description: Same team, having played Verbalizing the Where, Part 1 while seated, now gets up and actually plays the event (scene) through. Players no longer verbalize their actions as in Part 1, but speak only when dialogue is necessary.

Notes: 1. If focus of Part 1 of the game has worked for the players, the *Where* with space objects should now seem to become perceptible to all observers (the invisible will become visible).

2. It is not necessary that every detail covered in the narration be part of the scene played.

3. If the narrative part of this exercise has dealt with what players are thinking rather than on the detail of the physical realities around players, Part 2 can become no more than a "soap opera."

4. Note the complete absence of playwriting in these scenes as true improvisation appears.

Keep the physical sense of the Where—smells, colors, textures—communicate it!
Do not tell us in words!

Players, did the first part of this game help give life to the onstage situation in Part 2?
Was the playing of the event or scene easier because you talked it through before?
Audience players, after the actors got to their feet, was greater depth brought to the playing of the event or scene?
Was there more life than usual in improvised scenes?
More involvement and relation?
Players, do you agree?

Chapter 11:
COMMUNICATING WITH SOUNDS

The following pages contain a variety of games to stimulate and refine communication skills. Sound effects, gibberish, percussion, and extended sounds will now be added to players' tools for communication.

Gibberish

Gibberish games are extremely valuable and should be played throughout the workshops. Simply stated, gibberish is the substitution of shaped sounds for recognizable words. It should not be confused with "double talk," where actual words are inverted or mispronounced in order to scramble meaning. Nor is it a code language like Pig Latin or Alphalpha.

The meaning of a sound in gibberish will be understood only when the player conveys it by action, expressions, or tone of voice. (It is important that this should be left for the player to discover.)

Developing fluency in "no-symbol" speech brings with it a release from word patterns that may not come easily to some players. Demonstrate what gibberish is before using it in a game.

A teacher wrote us about his second grade bilingual classroom. "The children were restless. I began my lesson by addressing them in gibberish. ('Gallorusheo! Moolasay rallava plagee? Plinteeta fringtion drub sincta flu.') Suddenly, there was a big roar of laughter from the children. They could not understand a bit of my gibberish. Some children raised their hands. I thought they were going to ask me to explain why I was talking so strangely. But when I called on them, they responded in a fluent gibberish. Soon everyone was saying something. Not a word of explanation was necessary."

Because gibberish uses sounds of language minus the symbols (words), communication is put on a direct-experiential level for both other players and the audience. The player who shows the most resistance to gibberish is usually the person who interacts with others almost entirely through talk and shows great anxiety when told to be

□ *Gibberish is a vocal utterance accompanying an action, not the translation of an English phrase.*

□ *A scene that cannot be understood in gibberish is often nothing but verbal gags, plot, or ad-libbing. Gibberish develops the expressive physical language vital to stage life by removing the dependency on words alone to express meaning.*

quiet. When one anxiety-ridden student had an insight into gibberish she remarked, "You are on your own when you speak gibberish!" When asked if that wasn't also true when she used words, she thought for a moment and replied: "No, when you use words, people know the words you are saying. So you don't have to do anything yourself!"

Gibberish forces the player to show and not tell. Because the sounds are meaningless, the player has no way of camouflaging meaning. Physicalizing mood, problem, relation, and character becomes organic. Body tension is released, for players must listen and watch each other closely if they are to understand one another.

Ideas, terms, and phrases important to this chapter:

Nonverbal communication: Sometimes a way of making contact more profound than speech. (Note the decreasing use of dialogue in modern serious films.) Like the Mirror games and the Space Object games, the Gibberish series develops communication outside speech.

Off-balance moments: Opportunities to help players lose self-protective attitudes.

***Gibberish! English!* . . . (or *Gibberish! Spanish!* . . .):** Gives the player no time to think. Without a time lag, constructive off-balance moments will occur.

— GIBBERISH INTRODUCTION ——————————

Purpose: To be introduced to the possibilities in nonverbal communication.

Focus: On communicating in gibberish.

Description: Gibberish is the substitution of shaped sounds for recognizable words. Gibberish is a vocal utterance accompanying an action, not the translation of an English phrase or sentence. Ask the whole group to turn to neighbors and carry on conversations as if speaking an unknown language. Players should converse as if making perfect sense.

Notes: 1. Before presenting the concept to your class, practice use of gibberish with family or friends.

2. Keep the conversation going until everyone participates.

3. Have those who stick with a monotonous *dadeeda* sound with little lip movement converse with those who are more fluent in gibberish.

4. While most of the group will be delighted at their ability to speak to each other in gibberish, a few will be tied to speech for communication and will seem almost paralyzed, physically as well as vocally. Treat this casually and, in subsequent Gibberish games, flow of sound and body expression should become one.

5. The Gibberish series can be used in conjunction with a number of other games.

Use as many different sounds as possible!
Exaggerate your mouth movements!
Try chewing movements!
Vary the tone!
Keep usual speech rhythm!
Let the gibberish flow!

Was there variety in the gibberish?
Did gibberish flow?
Did it sound like conversation?

—— GIBBERISH: TEACHING ——————

Purpose: To communicate without real words.

Focus: On making contact.

Description: Teams of three to ten players. Team agrees on *Where, Who,* and *What* so that players are in a teaching-learning situation.

Examples: 1. *Where:* first-grade classroom, *Who:* teacher and students, *What:* learning to read; 2. an anatomy class; 3. airline hostess class. (You may want students to collaborate on a floor plan as in WHERE GAME WITH DIAGRAMS.)

Notes: 1. It will be apparent when communication is clear and, on the other hand, when players assume things or fill in for each other.

2. Unnecessary verbalizing becomes obvious when there is no apparent understanding among players.

3. This game contains elements of FOLLOW THE FOLLOWER.

Communicate to students!
Students, work with the teacher!

Did players communicate clearly to one another?
Players, do you agree?
How do people understand each other if they don't speak the same language?
How would you ask directions, for example, on a street in a Japanese city?

— GIBBERISH: SELLING —————————————————

Purpose: To sense the difficulty in persuading an audience.

Focus: On communicating to an audience.

Description: Single player, speaking gibberish, sells or demonstrates something to the audience. Allow one or two minutes clock time per player.

Notes: 1. Insist on direct contact. If players stare or look over the heads of the audience, ask them to "pitch" their sale, until the audience is actually seen. "Pitching," as practiced in carnivals or department stores, requires direct contact with others.

    2. Both audience and player will experience the difference when staring becomes seeing. An added depth, a certain quiet, will come into the work when this happens.

    3. Allow a player to be the timekeeper, who calls time at the halfway point and at the end.

Sell directly to us!
See us!
Share your gibberish!
Now pitch it!
Pitch it to us!

What was being sold or demonstrated?
Was there variety in the gibberish?
Did the player see us in the audience or stare at us?
Was there a difference between selling it and pitching it?

Think of a historical situation in which people communicated without a common language. How did the Indians teach the Pilgrims about the New World? How did the pilgrims explain where they had come from?

—— GIBBERISH/ENGLISH ——————————————

Purpose: To create an off-balance moment.

Focus: On communication.

Description: Teams of three — two players and a sidecoach. Players choose or accept a subject of conversation. When conversation begins to flow in English, sidecoach **Gibberish!**, and players are to change to gibberish until coached back to English. Conversation is to flow normally and to advance in meaning.

Notes: 1. GIBBERISH/ENGLISH is ideal for developing sidecoaching skills within all age ranges. When playing is understood, divide group into teams of three. Many teams, each with its own sidecoach, can play simultaneously. Give all team members a chance to sidecoach.

2. Regarding sidecoaching, if gibberish becomes confusing or embarrassing for any player, immediately change to English for a time. This helps the player who withdraws from the problem.

3. The moment of change should be when the player is off guard, in the middle of a thought or sentence. In the off-balance moment, the source of new insights — the intuitive — may be tapped.

4. This and other Gibberish games are useful in bilingual classrooms because they re-create, in play, experiences many students have been affected by.

Gibberish!
English!
Gibberish!
English! . . .

Did the conversation flow and have continuity?
Was communication maintained throughout?
Players, do you agree?

—— ECHO ——————————————————

Purpose: Exploration of sound for verbal and sensory agility.

Focus: On picking up and diminishing a sound without letting it stop.

Description: Two large teams. Players on a team stand one behind the other forming a column. The two columns face each other as if playing tug of war. First player in column 1 calls out a word or phrase. Starting with the first player in column 2 across the room, the word or phrase is repeated in turn by each succeeding player in column 2 without pause. Each player is to pick up the word or phrase and repeat it more softly so that the sound finally fades away at the end of the line. First player in column 2 then calls out a word or phrase for column 1 to echo, and the game continues back and forth between columns as before.

Let the sound flow through each of you!
Let sound slowly fade as it passes through you!
Each line is one body — one sound — the echo!

Did each succeeding player pick up the word without pause?
Did the sound flow as one echo?
Did it fade as an echo does?
What causes echoes in the natural world?

—— MIRROR SOUND ——————————————

Purpose: To communicate orally but nonverbally.

Focus: On mirroring partner's sounds.

Description: Teams of two players. Seated players face each other. One player is the initiator and makes sounds. The other player is the reflector and mirrors the sounds. When ***Change!*** is called, roles are reversed. The reflector becomes the initiator. The old initiator becomes the reflector who mirrors the new initiator's sounds. Change-overs must be made with no stop in the flow of sound.

Notes: 1. Sounds can be loud or soft, humming or shouting. Variety is desirable.

2. Teams of two players can gather in different spots around the room and all play this game simultaneously as teacher sidecoaches all teams at once.

3. As a variation, try this: Divide the group into teams of three. The third player becomes sidecoach to the other two. At a command from the teacher (***New sidecoach!***) the role of sidecoach goes to another player.

4. One hears an extension of this idea in both classical music and jazz. A theme or rhythm is played by one instrument and then repeated, with variations, by others.

No pause!
Notice your body/physical feeling as you mirror your partner's sound!
Change the mirror!
Keep the sound going!
Change!
Change!

—— FOREIGN LANGUAGE GIBBERISH——————

Purpose: To communicate fluently without words.

Focus: On communicating with another who does not speak the same language.

Description: Teams of two players. *Where, Who,* and *What* agreed upon, so that each player speaks a language which the other player does not understand. Both players use gibberish only.

Examples: Seeking a hotel or restaurant in a foreign country; haggling at a bazaar.

Note: Players should avoid imitating the rhythm and tone of any actual language—French, Swedish, German, for example—when doing their gibberish.

Variation: Divide the class into teams of four and subteams of two. Each team of four decides *Where, Who,* and *What.* For example, two students abroad seek information from officials at a foreign border.

Communicate to the other player!
You do not speak the same language! Communicate!

Variation:
Subteam A, you both speak the same language!
Subteam B, you understand each other!
Communicate with the foreigners!

What was happening? Where were players? Who were they?
Was it communicated directly or do you have to make up a story to fit the action?
Players, do you agree?

GIBBERISH INTERPRETER

Purpose: To communicate with and mirror other players using gibberish.

Focus: On following the follower with gibberish.

Description: Teams of two. One player speaks a foreign language and gives a speech or lecture to an audience (the class members) in gibberish. The second player understands the speaker's language and is the interpreter for the audience. Speaker pauses to let the interpreter translate what was said into English for audience understanding.

Variation: Teams of three. Two players speak different languages (both use gibberish). The third player understands both languages and acts as interpreter: the interpreter listens to one player and, turning to the other, translates what was communicated using English. The second player then responds to the first player's communication using gibberish, which the interpreter translates for the first player, again using English. (It may be helpful for the teams to establish *Where, Who,* and *What*: a customs office, a party for visiting diplomats, a border inspection, etc.) Conversation continues back and forth between the two foreigners through the interpreter, who always speaks English. (Two interpreters can also be used.)

Notes: 1. As there is nonverbal dialogue going on, the gibberish speakers and their interpreters will follow the follower.

2. Like other games in this series, this one is an adaptation of another game (FOLLOW THE FOLLOWER) using gibberish. Many such combinations are possible.

3. It is also an exercise of great entertainment value and has been used by a professional improvisation company.

Interpreter, know what is being communicated!
Know what the speaker is saying!
Follow the follower!

Players, did interpreter pass on what you communicated?
Interpreter player, were you following the follower?
Audience, do you agree?

— EXTENDED SOUND —————————————

Purpose: To heighten and extend theatrical experience by showing that sound (dialogue) occupies space.

Focus: On keeping the sound in space between players and letting it land in fellow player.

Description: Two or more partners sitting a distance apart.
    1. All players send a sound to all other players.
    2. Each player sends a sound to each fellow player.
    3. Give and take sending a sound to fellow players.

Note: This game is useful in early rehearsals of a production rehearsal period.

No words! Keep the sound between you!
Keep the body upright!
Send forth the souund!
Keep the sound in the space!
Let the sound land! Extend the souuund! Sloooow motion!
Speed it up as fast as you can!
Normal speed! Keep the space between you!
Extennnnd the souuuund!
Give and take!

Variation:
Long distance!

Did players keep the sound in the space between them?
Did the sound land?
Did players give and take?

Chapter 12:
MULTIPLE-STIMULUS GAMES

To achieve survival in our complex society, individuals must handle, integrate, and work with a variety of incoming data. Whether one is driving a car, flying a jet, or just crossing a busy street, attention is, of necessity, divided. At the same time, everything must be simultaneously integrated, coordinated, and selected for harmony, unity, well-being, and safety.

Although most games automatically involve the handling of multiple stimuli, specific games particularly heighten skills in this area. All of the following require the student to open up and respond to many incoming stimuli simultaneously. You may feel that Multiple-Stimulus games will create anxiety in players, but they do not if played in a spirit of adventure. The players will build an ever-increasing capacity for, and strength in, dealing with a multitude of phenomena. The sidecoach is responsible for keeping the spirit of adventure operating in these games.

□ *Players grow agile and alert, ready and eager for any unusual play as they respond to many random happenings simultaneously.*

Phrases important to this chapter:

Give and take!: Like *Follow the follower!*, synchronizes players when coached successfully.

Two scenes!: Creates two centers, clears confusion.

— HOW MUCH DO YOU REMEMBER? ———

Purpose: To concentrate on two activities at once.

Focus: On reading and listening at the same time.

Description: Count off into teams of two players — a reader and a talker. The reader starts to silently read any story or article from a book or magazine while the talker relates some incident or past experience directly to the reader. Reader is to focus on being open to both what he is reading and what the talker is telling him. Before reversing roles, reader tells talker what he read and what he heard.

Notes: 1. This exercise can be played with a group of pairs working simultaneously or on an individual basis.

2. For inexperienced players, it is suggested that the subject matter of the reading be kept light and fairly easy. It can become more difficult and technical as the players gain confidence and skill.

(To reader): *Can you recall anything your partner said? Can you remember more of what you read or more of what your partner was talking about?*

— THREE-WAY CONVERSATION ———

Purpose: To develop alertness to multiple incoming data.

Focus: For center player, to hold two conversations simultaneously; for end players, to hold a single conversation with center player only.

Description: Three seated players. One player (A) is the center; the others (B and C) are the ends.

    B (end)   A (center)   C (end)

Each end player chooses a topic and engages the center in conversation as if the other end player did not exist. Center must converse with both ends, fluent in both conversations (responding and initiating when necessary) without excluding either end player. In effect, the center holds one conversation on two topics. End players converse with center player only.

Notes: 1. Rotate players by sidecoaching **Next!** New players, one at a time, come up and take an end seat, bumping one end player to the center, while the center moves over to become the other end player.

2. Center player does not just respond to end players, but can also initiate conversation.

3. Players will best avoid questions. Questions tend to create two separate conversations instead of two simultaneous conversations.

Speak and hear at the same time! Take your time! No questions! No sharing of information!

Did players avoid asking questions? Did A stop hearing one player while speaking to the other? Did end players pick up from each other? Did center player also begin conversation?

—— THREE-WAY WRITING ——

Purpose: To learn to concentrate on several things simultaneously.

Focus: On writing about three different subjects at the same time.

Description: Full group, seated at tables or desks. Each player divides a large piece of paper into three columns and marks them 1, 2, and 3, with the name of a different subject at the top of each column. When the sidecoach calls out that column number, player immediately (without pause) starts to write about the subject in that column. When another column number is called out, player stops (even in mid-word) and immediately starts to write about the subject for that column number in the column. Sidecoach will move from column number to column number randomly, and players are to pick up where they left off. When the game is over, each player should have a piece of paper with three different short essays or stories on it, none of them necessarily completed.

Notes: 1. THREE-WAY WRITING will produce an off-balance moment within which the player begins to act instinctively.

2. You will find this a good game for incorporating curriculum needs by choosing three topics the students are currently working with and having them all write on these topics. It will then begin to resemble the real-life experience of homework.

3. In early work with this exercise, try not to rush players, but do not go so slowly that time lag is allowed through which penmanship and spelling fears become censors to the content. After the game is called for time, players can be given additional time to edit for spelling and to neatly rewrite the final pieces.

4. This game is related to the traditional parlor game GUGGENHEIM.

Variation: In THREE-WAY DRAWING, students number three separate sheets of paper, title each with a topic name, and draw a simple picture on each, switching pages when new numbers are called.

One!
Three!
Two!
One!
Two!
Three!
. . . Don't pause to finish the sentence!
Move to the new column right away!
Keep writing!
Forget about spelling!
Forget about writing neatly!

— DRAWING OBJECTS GAME ———————

Purpose: To communicate an object quickly through drawing it.

Focus: On communicating through images.

Description: Compile a list of objects with simple but outstanding characteristics (train, cow, cat, Christmas tree, etc.). Divide the group into two teams by counting off in twos. Each team is at an equal distance from the leader, who has a prepared list of objects. Each team sends a player to the leader, who shows both players the same word simultaneously. For nonreaders, the leader whispers the word to each player. Players run back to their respective teams and communicate the word through drawing the object so their teammates can identify it. The first team to identify and call out the object wins a point. Continue as before with two more players and a new word until each team member has had a chance to draw an object.

Notes: 1. Artistic ability is unimportant since this is a game of spontaneous selectivity that shows which students can quickly make a visual communication. Artists within a group are often less facile than nonartists.

2. The drawings can be made on large sheets of drawing paper with crayon or felt pen or on chalkboards.

3. You will note that points and the score become unimportant in the excitement of playing.

4. All age groups love this game. From time to time, allow your students to bring in their own lists and lead the game.

5. In many civilizations, such as those of China or Ancient Egypt, systems of writing were developed in which each word was represented by a picture. Students playing this game may enjoy imagining that they are inventing writing.

Variation (For advanced players): Use abstract words (joy, melancholy, triumph, generosity, energy, etc.). Synonyms count as correct identifications.

Communicate!
Keep drawing!
This is not a guessing game!

Chapter 13:
PUPPETRY

Playmaking for Parts of the Body

These games are designed to develop more organic, better integrated use of the feet and legs. They are also a natural lead-in to puppetry and shadow plays. For an almost instant puppet show in your classroom, have players play HANDS ALONE. Then, have players perform the same game with socks over their hands. Socks can be decorated with hair, ears, beards, hats, or whatever intrigues the players.

If you are interested in pursuing puppetry further with your players, there is much useful material available at libraries and bookstores on the history and construction of puppets. (See Bibliography, Part B.) From the simple sock puppet described above, to elementary rod and shadow puppets, to very sophisticated marionettes and Bunraku puppets, introducing puppetry to the classroom drama class can be very rewarding, expanding students' notions of the nature of theater.

☐ *If players solve the problems of showing* Where, Who, *and* What *with their feet, or hands, or back alone, they will have gone a long way toward discovering the use of focus in puppetry.*

A Quick Curtain in the Classroom

A curtain, screen, or cloth is needed for these games.[1] It should be hung just high enough to show the feet and legs of the players or — when playing HANDS ALONE — dropped so players can raise their hands above it. (It is also possible to play HANDS ALONE by cutting slits in the curtain and having players push hands through them.)

Two eye hooks should be fastened in abutting walls equidistant from the corner. They should be six to seven feet above the floor. Connect them with a waxed wire. (Waxing the wire will help the curtain move more smoothly.) With a suitable number of sheets sewn together and fitted with simple curtain hooks at the top, even the least mechanical classroom teacher can create a quick backdrop for theater-game workshop playing.

This same backdrop, with the bottom pinned up, can be used to play FEET AND LEGS ALONE. Two additional eye hooks, set 18 to 24 inches closer to the floor, can be

[1]It is also necessary for TELEVISION SCREEN and SHADOW SCREEN, which follow.

used to hang the curtain lower to create a visual stage for puppet plays and HANDS ALONE. (In determining the height of the puppet curtain, consider whether players will do their puppet shows in a kneeling or a standing position.)

The same backdrop, if backlit with a strong light, can become the shadow screen for other games. Make sure there is space behind the screen for players and their shadow puppets.

— FEET & LEGS ALONE #1 —

Purpose: To discover the possibilities in communicating through only one part of the body.

Focus: On showing *Who* and *What* and/or a mood with the feet and legs alone.

Show who you are with your toes!
Put all that energy into your feet!
We cannot see your face!
Put your feeling in your feet!

Description: One at a time, each player is to show, without speech, either *Who, What,* or a mood (impatience, grief, etc.) using only feet and legs.

Notes: 1. This exercise, like others isolating parts of the body, helps players physicalize the sidecoaching used in many of these theater games:
Feel the anger in the small of your back!
Hear the sound with your fingertips!
Taste the food all the way down to your toes!

2. The phrase *See it with your toes!*, for instance, helps players transcend cerebral concepts of a feeling and restore that feeling to the total organism.

3. Students may be frustrated by the limitations placed on them by this game. It can be pointed out that all performing arts limit the full range of human behavior. As a rule, opera singers don't dance. Ballet dancers don't sing or even talk on stage. Sports also limit players. What would happen if a tennis player caught the ball or if a baseball player tackled an opponent? What if a football player took a bat or a racket on the field?

What state of being was communicated?
What was the player doing?
Could the expression have been stronger?
More varied?

— FEET & LEGS ALONE #2 ———————————

Purpose: To collaborate with another player in communicating something to an audience despite restricted movement.

Focus: On communicating with feet and legs alone.

Description: A screen or curtain is set up as in game #1. Two players agree on *Where, Who,* and *What.* No dialogue is to be used. Relationships, feelings, *Where,* etc. are to be communicated by the feet alone.

Examples: Old friends meeting at a playground or watching TV. A grandmother refusing a salesman at the door.

Notes: 1. The number of players can be increased after the problem is solved in twos.

2. Encourage players to work barefoot when possible. Knowing their feet are exposed, players will work with greater expressiveness.

Heighten it!
Show us what is happening through your feet!

Who were players?
Where?
How old?
Was communication clear?
Was there variety of movement?

— HANDS ALONE ——————————————

Purpose: To isolate the hands as an expressive tool of the body.

Focus: On showing *Where, Who,* and *What* by means of the hands alone.

Description: Teams of two or more players agree on *Where, Who,* and *What,* which is communicated to audience with hands alone.

Notes: 1. Players should be hidden from view so that only hands and forearms show. A puppet stage or table curtained off is sufficient.

2. For shadow play, a projector with light turned on against a wall or screen can also be used, with players silhouetting hands against screen.

3. Actual hand props may be used for this exercise but are not essential to its effectiveness.

4. The tendency to plan a story is strong in this exercise. Players may have to be reminded to let the focus work for them.

5. It may interest older students if you point out to them that many forms of live theater force restrictions on the performer: Greek tragedy and Kabuki cover the actors' faces with masks. Balinese puppet theater (show them a picture if possible) is a highly developed art form. Audiences accept these customs quickly. For example, it requires three men to operate a single Japanese Bunraku puppet. No puppet stage hides their bodies. But after a few minutes, all eyes are on the puppet alone.

Laugh with your fingers!
Shrug your hands, not your shoulders!
Put all your energy into your fingertips!
Let focus on hands move you!
Put your face in no motion!

Who, What, *and* Where *were players?*
Did players show with hands?
Players, did you plan the story or did it grow out of involvement in the Where, Who, *and* What?
Did hands communicate feelings, age, relationships, etc.?

—— EXERCISE FOR THE BACK ——

Purpose: To communicate with the whole body.

Focus: On using the back to show feeling or a state of being.

Description: Single player chooses an activity that requires sitting with back to the audience, such as playing the piano, doing homework, etc. Player is to communicate feeling or attitude with the back alone.

Note: Lead in to this game by having two players stand before a group. One faces front, the other turns away. Have group list parts of the body which can be used for communication. Ask players to move the part called. Front view: movable forehead, eyebrows, eyes, cheeks, nose, mouth, jaw, tongue, shoulders, chest, stomach, hands and feet, knees, etc. Back view: head (no movable parts), shoulders, torso (solid mass), heels, backs of legs (comparatively immobile). Compare the number of movable (communicating) parts of the body when facing or turned away from the audience.

Keep the feeling in your back! Not on your face!

Did player show with the back? Could more variety of movement be found? Was Who *communicated? Age?*

—— TOTAL BODY INVOLVEMENT ——

Purpose: To test (and demonstrate) the effectiveness of games focusing on parts of the body.

Focus: On head-to-foot, full-body involvement.

Description: After any game or series of games using a part of the body, divide the group into teams. Play any PART OF A WHOLE game with *Where, Who,* and *What* agreed upon. This sidecoaching places emphasis on another aspect of the playing.

Examples: For *Where,* use Super Bowl bleachers, a sunken pirate ship visited by deep-sea divers. For *What,* try ants removing a pebble from the mouth of the ant hill, a space ship beyond the pull of gravity, working at a car wash, inventing a cure for the cold in a laboratory, etc.

Notes: 1. Many mannerisms will have disappeared. For instance, players who previously relied on facial grimaces will, in many cases, lose this limitation as a result of these exercises.

2. The *Where, Who,* and *What* may, ideally, be taken from something being studied in another field.

— PUPPETS ON STRINGS ————————————

Purpose: To discover the wide range of expression possible even to a marionette.

Focus: On moving like puppets.

Description: Teams of two or more players agree upon *Where*, *Who*, and *What*. Players are to go through *Where*, *Who*, and *What* moving limbs and whole bodies as if they were controlled like string puppets. If possible, demonstrate marionette movement with an actual puppet on strings.

Notes: 1. Younger children are delighted by this game.

2. The *Where*, *Who*, and *What* need not be connected with puppetry. Puppetlike movements are the focus of the game only.

3. If an actual puppet demonstration is not possible, give time for a short discussion of such movements before playing.

Move your jaw like a puppet!
Your elbows!
Knees!
Sit!
Walk!
Gesture like puppets!
Work with one another!

Did players maintain puppet-like movements throughout?
Players, do you agree?

— PARTS OF THE BODY/FULL SCENE ————

Purpose: To develop ease in focusing on several areas of the body as expressive instruments.

Focus: On a part of the body (given by sidecoach) within *Where*, *Who*, and *What*.

Description: Teams of three or four players agree on *Where*, *Who*, and *What*. In turn, just before playing, each team is given a part of the body for focus. Players allow focus on that part of the body to move them through *Where*, *Who*, and *What* in full view of audience players.

Notes: 1. Play this game after students are familiar with all previous games which isolate movement.

2. Note that many distracting personal mannerisms will disappear after doing this series of exercises.

Keep focus on hands, feet, back . . .! (whatever was given)
Show it with ———! (the part given as focus)

Did players let focus move them or did they just add the part of the body to Where, Who, *and* What?
Players, do you agree?
Did focus on parts of the body bring more spontaneity to players' work?
Players, did holding focus give you a freedom of response?

Chapter 14:
PLAYMAKING FOR RADIO, TELEVISION, AND FILM

Puppetry limits tools of expression to certain parts of the body (see the preceding chapter). Radio and television impose other limitations. Films have fewer restrictions but use a number of conventions to convey ideas, develop characters, and express moods.

The following exercises are intended not to train players specifically for these media, but to focus energies within the limitations of each. The television games restrict players to use of their upper bodies. In the radio games the players work on the problem of using voices only to communicate to an audience. They must be able to select those things which will allow the audience to see the story "through their ears." Other games show the vital importance of sound track, montage, etc., to television and films.

In radio games, the scenes take place behind the curtain, since we are concerned with the voices alone. If no curtain is available, the audience may turn their backs to the playing area. Each improvisation should have one or two players doing nothing but opening and closing doors, moving chairs, ringing bells, howling like the wind, etc. Sound effects are not to be planned any more than dialogue.

A microphone, amplifier, and speaker are useful for radio games. It is even more important to rig up a sound table with bells, buzzers, a rain box, a door, a box of broken glass, a newspaper, chalk and blackboard, a tape player and tapes. You will always find a few students who are talented at providing vocal sound effects.

For preliminary work in all media, a short discussion on radio (the most limiting of the forms) is advisable, so that players will be able to clarify what they are trying to do. The problem of showing rather than telling in this medium is more challenging, even, than in television.

"When you listen to a story on the radio, what happens?"

The answer will arrive eventually: "The listener sees the story."

"Then, when you do a radio play, what are you trying to do?"

□ *The focus in these games is to show* Where, Who, *and* What *by voice and sound alone (without telling).*

"Let the audience see the story in their minds."

"How can a classroom be shown by the use of sound and voice alone."

"By making classroom sounds."

"Give some examples."

"Chalk could squeak on the board. Someone could use the pencil sharpener." "A lot of chairs could be pushed back." "A lunch bell rings."

"In a television show or a film, how can we show that a woman and a boy are mother and son?"

"The boy could come in and say, 'Hello . . . I'm back from the store. Can I go out and play now?' "

☐ *A discussion along the lines of those held during* Where *sessions will stimulate players to find many sounds especially pertinent to a classroom, kitchen, or living room.*

— RADIO

Purpose: To learn to select those things which will help the audience to experience the story "through their ears."

Focus: To show *Who* by voice and sound alone.

Description: Three or more players. *Who* decided upon. Each actor makes list of the characteristics he or she is attempting to convey: age, weight, temperament, appearance, etc. Players then improvise a scene using voice and sound effects alone. The members of the audience are to make their own list of characteristics as the action progresses. When playing is over, lists are compared.

Notes: 1. Try to prevent actors from taking on the role of narrator. When students put their minds to solving *Where* and *Who*, narration will not be necessary.

2. The focus can be changed to: showing *Where.* Here individual characterizations will be less important and background sound will be more elaborate.

3. The radio and television exercises are intended not to train the actor specifically for radio or television but to focus his or her energies within the limitations of each medium. RADIO should be played periodically to help solve acting and story problems in production.

Audience, did actors show us Where *and* Who *by sound and voice alone?*

—— Greek Chorus ——————————

Purpose: To support stage action vocally.

Description: Choose a children's singing game and have the chorus sing the verses as the actors act them out. A section of the chorus may also do sound effects, such as wind, birds, etc.

Examples: Princess Thorn Rosa, The Mulberry Bush.

Note: Classical Greek choruses also danced while singing and commenting on the action of the play.

—— Vocal Sound Effects ——————

Purpose: To create an environment using sounds.

Focus: On becoming the environment (*Where*) through sound effects alone.

Description: Teams of four to six players agree on *Where*. Using sound as part of a whole, players become the chosen environment (a railroad station, jungle, harbor, etc.). Because there is no onstage action, players may stand out of sight of audience, or audience players may close eyes.

Notes: 1. This game (like Choral Reading) is designed for use with a classroom microphone, though it may be played without one.

2. A tape recording of a team's work played back during evaluation adds to everyone's awakening. Excitement results when players recognize their individual contributions as part of the whole.

3. Allow use of cellophane crackling for fire, a straw in a glass of water for streams, etc. Encourage variety.

4. If a mike is available, pass it around, allowing individual children to experiment with sound effects.

(Usually not needed.)
Sound is your fellow player!
Bring the **Where** *into the space!*
Give the sounds their place in space!
Each sound is part of the whole!

Where were the players?
Was the **Where** *in the space or in the players' heads?*
(Ask individuals):
Were you part of the whole?

— POISON★ —————————————————————————————

Purpose: To make players attentive to music.

Focus: On the music.

Description: A piano or tape deck is adequate to provide music. The players stand in a circle and pass an object from one to another while the music is being played. Whoever has it when the music stops is "poisoned" and drops out of the game. However, the poisoned player may try to stay in the game by passing the object to the next player even after the music stops. If the latter takes it, he or she is out. If the group is large, four or five objects may be started at different places in the circle to make the game move more quickly. When the circle is reduced to ten or fifteen players, all but one of the objects may be taken out.

Variation: If no piano or tape deck is available, the teacher can face away from the players singing a simple, familiar tune. The teacher stops abruptly. Whoever is caught with the object now becomes conductor. The teacher in turn becomes the orchestra. He or she faces the players while the poisoned player conducts the orchestra, facing away from the other players. Each new conductor is allowed to change the tune. The conductor, in turn, stops the music abruptly. The player newly caught now becomes the conductor and the previous conductor joins the teacher in the orchestra. Play continues until only one player remains.

Notes: 1. Children love playing conductor. The variation on this game removes the sense of failure from being caught and creates full involvement.

2. This traditional game is an ideal lead-in to other games requiring a chorus, like CHORAL READING.

—— TELEVISION SCREEN ————————————

Purpose: For audience: to introduce students to the conventions of TV shows.

Focus: For players: on agility in changing character, costumes, and content.

Description: Cut a large opening in a cardboard box or build an actual oversized TV frame for the actors to play behind. Set up a well-supplied costume rack and prop table. One team will be the actors; one team will be the family (audience). Actors go behind the frame. Family members are seated in "living room," facing screen, where they have gathered for an evening of TV. Each member of the family calls out his or her favorite show, goes to the TV screen, and "turns on the set." The actors must play the show called for. The game can be made more fun (and more difficult) if individual family members whisper the name of a show to the actors and the rest of the family must guess what it is. The family may "change the channel" or call for a new show at any time. The actors never know when they are going to be "shut off."

Notes: 1. Set-up should be extremely well organized, so that the TV actors can obtain their costumes and props.

2. After a time, switch the teams around so that students have an opportunity to play both actors and family.

3. The scenes, for the most part, will center on take-offs on current TV shows.

4. The chief value in this game is in continuing the discussion that arises from the evaluation questions.

Audience, how did actors let you know what program you were watching?
Did they show you who they were with their whole bodies?
Could you see more than their faces?
How many people fit on the screen?
How did they indicate Where?
Time of day?
Weather?
Do you always know the time and temperature in a TV show?
Players, did you feel cramped by the size of the screen?
What part of the body did you focus on?

— SHADOW SCREEN (MONTAGE) —

Purpose: To explore what can be communicated by physical action (gesture) alone.

Focus: On working within the limitations imposed by the screen.

Description: Same teams as in TELEVISION SCREEN. Set up a large shadow screen, 6 feet by 4 feet (see description in Puppetry). Have on hand a well-stocked costume rack and box full of props. Here, actors go behind screen and act out scenes or shows as in TELEVISION SCREEN. But they are seen by the "family" only in silhouette. When actors and audience become comfortable with the limitations, have them continue to play *without* dialogue.

Notes: 1. As in the previous game, the value of this is in developing the discussion begun by the evaluation questions.

2. Students may not have seen much shadow play but they will be familiar with the photomontage commonly used in feature films, which use action, setting, and no dialogue to tell a story.

Audience, how did you know what was happening?
Did the dialogue help?
Was it necessary?
Did you see any actions you didn't understand?
Players, what were you showing?
Audience, how could the action have been made clearer?
Do you always hear actors talking in movies?
If actors in movies don't talk, how do you know what they're thinking?
How do you know what they want?
What they need?

— SOUNDTRACK —

Purpose: To establish a background (environment) supporting a scene.

Focus: On following the follower with sound effects.

Description: Teams of six or more players agree on *Where, Who,* and *What*. Half the team will be playing onstage; the other half will be gathered in a small group and vocally make all sound effects needed by the onstage playing. (If a small classroom microphone is available, these players should use it.) Onstage players keep up their own dialogue. Players are to let sound effects and onstage activity connect by following the follower.

Notes: 1. Take time to have the full group experience both onstage and backstage positions.

2. You will find your players very versatile in using the human vocal equipment to produce a wide variety of sound effects. Doors shut, creak; a car starts, stops; brakes screech; people walk, run, knock on doors; winds blow; coffee cups or glasses clink. The list is endless. Whatever is needed for the stage action will emerge.

Follow the follower!
Don't lead off!
Onstage players, don't get ahead of soundtrack!
Soundtrack, don't get ahead of players!
Follow the starter!
Follow the follower in sound!

Audience, did sound effects and onstage activity become as one?
Players, do you agree?
Did sound effects help the scene?
How does the soundtrack work in movies and TV?
What is the effect of the laughtrack?
What does the background music tell us?

— CHORAL READING —

Purpose: To support stage action with sounds and other effects.

Focus: Chorus: on following the conductor; Players: on establishing *Who, What,* and *Where* by following the follower; Conductor: on keeping the connection between chorus and players in constant progression.

Description: A large team agrees on *Who, What,* and *Where* and divides itself into three sections: onstage players, a conductor, and a choral group. The choral group stands or sits to one side of the playing area. The group agrees on various sound effects needed for the chosen scene and is subdivided into parts, like sections of an orchestra, each of which creates a different sort of audible support. (For example, a scene set in a forest might include sections that provide sound for birds, wind, wild animals, echoes, as well as hummers, singers, and/or whistlers to establish a mood.) Before starting, give the conductor time to practice with the "orchestra," cuing sections by pointing to them and heightening or lowering the intensity of sounds by raising and lowering his or her arms. Onstage players begin. The conductor leads the choral group in supplying background effects and is the connection between onstage players and the choral group.

Notes: 1. VOCAL SOUND EFFECTS and POISON are the natural lead-ins to this game.

2. The presence of a conductor helps to do away with any fragmentation. An intense involvement is required to keep an ensemble moving. Allow many or all to have the experience of conducting. To make this possible, it may be necessary to change the conductor during playing. This can be done without stopping the playing by sidecoaching *New conductor!*

3. If possible, record the group effort and let everyone hear the playback.

4. While we associate this sort of division of labor with modern media, it has very deep roots in traditional theater as well. Anyone who has ever seen Japanese theater or that of other Asian cultures will have been struck by the presence of onstage musicians providing sound effects and sometimes delivering the lines for the actor/dancers or puppets performing the scene.

— DUBBING —

Purpose: To improve (nonverbal) communication and increase sensory awareness in a media setting.

Focus: On following the follower, with the voice of one player and the movements of another becoming as one whole (single) player.

Description: Two or three players (Subteam A) choose players of same sex to be their voices (Subteam B). This whole team (Subteam A plus Subteam B) agrees on *Where, Who,* and *What.* The voice players gather around a microphone with a clear view of the playing area, where the body players go through *Where, Who,* and *What.* The voice players reflect the onstage activity through the dialogue. The body players move their lips as if speaking, but are to use silent gibberish — no attempt to mouth exact words! Both subteams follow the follower (see FOLLOW THE FOLLOWER) in voice and action. Have the voice and body players exchange places and continue the same *Where, Who,* and *What* or choose a new one.

Notes: 1. At first, the separate players will become one body/one voice only in flashes, but when the connection is made, a burst of power rises between and through players, uniting them in true relation. Allow ten minutes of playing time before reversing teams.

2. If this connection does not take place and the voice simply follows the body's moves or vice versa, play more Mirror and Space games, until players experience what happens when they don't initiate, but follow the initiator, who is also following.

3. Sidecoaching is born out of what is emerging. The teacher does not demand, but acts as a fellow player, exploring and heightening what is seen and emerging.

4. When voice becomes one with onstage player's actions, the onstage player gets a sense of having actually spoken the words. Onstage players are not to be used as puppets by the dubbers; time must be allowed for onstage activity to emerge.

5. When dubbing works, two players experience true union and become as one player.

Stay with each other!
Avoid anticipating what will be said!
Reflect only what you hear!
Move your mouth in silent gibberish!
Follow each other!
Become one voice!
One body!

Players, did voice and body become as one?
Audience, do you agree?

Chapter 15:
DEVELOPING MATERIAL

Although theater games are invaluable in the preparation of scripted theater pieces, they have traditionally been associated with improvisation, storytelling, and story theater. This chapter and the ones following contain a variety of exercises, commentaries, and games that lead players from workshop to public performance.

☐ *Improvisation and story theater tap the intuitive energies of the player rather than subordinate them to the dictates of the playwright and script.*

Improvisation

Taking suggestions from the audience can be a delightful part of a theater program and quickly makes the audience part of the game. Agility and speed in getting a character, setting up *Where*, and selecting an acting problem are necessary to the success of the scene. All such games should be used continuously in the workshops (the Who games are especially useful). Many of the exercises in the book can be used exactly as they are done in workshops, with exhilarating results.

The following games show how scenes can be built from very simple premises.

☐ *Players should try to build on an action or problem and not a story or joke, otherwise many of the audience's suggestions fizzle as players struggle to be "funny."*

— BOX FULL OF HATS —————————————

Purpose: To rapidly establish a character (*Who*).

Focus: On selecting costume pieces for character quality.

Description: Teams of two or more players. Players agree on *Where*, *Who*, and *What* and then pick costume pieces from the box full of hats to fit the scene. Alternatively, players may pick costume pieces at random, allow the costumes to suggest character qualities, and then choose *Where*, *Who*, and *What* based on their selections.

Notes: 1. Your box of hats is simply as many costumes, costume pieces, and small props as you can readily collect: old gowns, jackets, a chef's hat, a sailor's cap, an Indian headdress, helmets, shawls, capes, blankets, sheets, paper wings, tails for animals, gloves, canes, eyeglasses, pipes, umbrellas, etc. A prop table might display: balloons, feathers, chains, a jumping rope, bell, ball, rubber band, bean bag, horn, egg beater, triangle, party toys, etc. Hang clothing, blankets, and sheets on a rack with the box full of hats nearby. Old neckties can be used as belts, making it possible to use any size dress or coat by taking up extra length and girth.

    2. This game reflects an old tradition. In the theater of Shakespeare's time, troupes included only about a dozen to sixteen actors (all men and boys). Most had to play several different roles in a single play. Audiences distinguished characters by what they wore.

Example: In a typical scene developed by slightly older children, players chose to be a Rich Bird, a Bird Lover, an Explorer, a Princess, a Friend, a Dog, and a Queen. The story: The Explorer, with his Dog, was hunting for birds in the jungle. He caught a rare Rich Bird, and brought it back to his employer, the Bird Lover, who took it to show to the Queen, the Princess, and her Friend. The Dog, who disliked the Rich Bird, came along too.

Variations: 1. Once players have randomly selected and donned costumes, audience players determine *Where*, *Who*, and *What* for players.

    2. In ANIMAL IMAGES, an exercise which originated with Maria Ouspenskaya, the characters must all be animals (though they retain speech and other human qualities). A number of plays have used such characters (from the nineteenth-century farce *Loves of a Cat* to the Broadway musical *Cats*).

Share your voice!
Keep objects in space — out of the head!
Show! Don't tell!
Become part of the whole!
One minute to play!

Audience, did costume pieces help the players' Where, Who, *and* What?
Did the objects follow the action?
Players, do you agree?

— SKITS & SONGS ★ ——————————

Description: Dramatizable situations, such as a sporting goods shop in summer; catching the bus to school in the morning; or lunch time in a nursery are written on slips of paper of different color. These slips are then cut into several pieces, shaken up in a hat, and distributed among the players, who seek out their groups by matching the colors of their papers. When all the groups are assembled, one player, acting as master of ceremonies, calls upon the various groups to act their scenes. Songs may be substituted for dramatizable situations, and may be sung, or sung and dramatized simultaneously. Or, the song may be dramatized by one group, while the other groups try to name it.

— ON THE SPOT ——————————

Purpose: To train players in developing immediate responses to suggestion.

Focus: On developing a scene by combining bits of information.

Description: Each player writes on individual slips of paper a *Who, Where, What*, time, and weather. These slips are put into piles or containers according to the categories. Players then count off into teams of four or more. Each player picks a slip from the *Who* pile and each team takes one slip from each of the other piles. Each team immediately improvises a scene.

Variation: Audience vocally gives a *Where, Who, What*, etc. to a group of four to six. The team prepares the scene in front of the audience, who are thus made part of the game.

Notes: 1. The method of writing on slips of paper to set up a situation can be used with many other exercises.

2. Audiences for nearly a half-century have been excited by improvisational theater. Even if a skit does not come off as a story, it is exciting to watch the energy released by actors in the process of solving problems.

3. RADIO is a good lead-in to this game.

Was the scene set up quickly? Actors, what could have been done to speed the process? Audience, do you have other suggestions?

— CHARADES —————————————

Purpose: To develop dramatic material.

Focus: On obscuring a word within a series of events (scenes).

Description: Count off into teams of four to six players. Each team secretly selects a word such as "industrial," "monkey," "mistake," etc. and divides it into syllables. *Where, Who,* and *What* are agreed upon and an event (scene) played for each syllable and for the whole word. The audience players try to guess the word only after all the events (scenes) have been played out. At no time is the word itself or the syllable to be mentioned verbally.

Variation: Instead of giving free rein in choice of event (scene), the sidecoach provides specific themes on which each syllable must be based (political, scientific, current events, historical, fantasy, etc.).

Notes: 1. This is a time-consuming game as each team plays one, two, or three events (scenes). It might be advisable to have one or two teams play during a week, and the others in succeeding weeks.

2. Remind players to disregard the spelling of a word and think of the sound sense of a syllable: "mistake" could become "miss" + "take" or "mist" + "ache."

3. This game awakens players to a great variety of choices for *Where, Who,* and *What.*

4. Hats, capes, etc. collected for a classroom costume box add greatly to this game.

5. This game lends itself well to curriculum studies.

What was the word?
What was the first syllable?
The second?
Players, was the word or syllable ever mentioned?

Interpretation

The dramatic interpretation of short poems can also be used in public performance. Pieces of this sort should be based on rhythmic-movement games and those using space objects. The singing games in the book give examples of the way texts may be illustrated line by line through stage action.

But short poems may also be used as a basis for a stage action, scenes, or pantomime. In this case it will be more interesting for player and audience both if the poem is read and the player then uses it as a premise for action. (Sidecoach **Show! Don't tell!**)

Two examples of poems used successfully in theater-game workshops are the following, the first by Sandburg, the second by Dickinson. See the Bibliography, Part D, for many more resources.

"Fog"
The fog comes
on little cat feet

It sits looking
over harbor and city
on silent haunches
and then moves on.

☐ *Let a team perform this, each player working independently to interpret the piece in his or her own way.*

"I'm Nobody"
I'm nobody! Who are you?
Are you nobody, too?
Then there's a pair of us — don't tell!
They'd banish us, you know.

How dreary to be somebody!
How public, like a frog
To tell your name the livelong day
To an admiring bog!

☐ *This is most easily done by a minimum of three to four players:*
a. Nobody #1
b. Nobody #2
c. Frog
(d. Bog)

Building a Story

Building a Story games focus, at the beginning, on the word. (Begin this sequence with the Handwriting games as warm-ups and play some of the word games in Chapter 10 before beginning work on stories.) The following two games also help players focus on single words.

It is also possible to develop a story from the random selection of words. If students keep individual collections of vocabulary cards or personal word boxes, use these words to play. Otherwise, before dividing into teams, have each player write a half-dozen random, familiar words on slips of paper or 3×5 cards. Each player collects his or her cards into an envelope. Teams of three or more gather in different areas and play simultaneously. The players agree on a first player who spreads out his or her collection of word cards so that all teammates can see. Working together, arranging and rearranging the word cards, players build one story that includes all the words. (As an alternative, teams may shuffle together one-third of the cards from each of the envelopes.) If connecting words are needed, players write them on new cards or slips of paper and place them in context. The teacher should simply move from group to group, helping players spell and write new words or stimulating the organization of the story.

When the first story is completed and includes all the original words, the first player writes out the story on a piece of paper and gathers both original and new cards into his or her envelope. The next player spreads out his or her own selection of words and the team proceeds as above, building a story.

Read all the finished stories aloud.

—— Spelling ★ ————————————————

Purpose: A different approach to communication.

Focus: On communicating to another player.

Description: Whole group breaks into teams of two or three. They hold conversations, spelling their words.

Notes: 1. Continue as long as spirits are high and all conversing is fluent. The excitement of a connection with fellow players will appear.

2. After players are familiar with the game, choose a small section of a script or story to read by spelling. If your group finds this difficult, do not spend a long time with it.

Feel yourself spelling!
See the letters!

How much of the conversation was understood by the listener?
Did the speller see the letters?

—— Vowels & Consonants ★ ————————————

Purpose: To suggest a different approach to the spoken word.

Focus: On contacting the vowels or consonants in a word as it is spoken.

Description: Six or eight players stand in a circle or in two lines facing each other. Each player is to begin a quiet conversation with the player opposite (eight players means four simultaneous conversations). Players are to focus on either the vowels or consonants as sidecoached in the words they speak without putting emphasis on them or changing speech patterns. Keeping voices low, players are to move back away from each other as far as space permits, then forward again as sidecoached.

Notes: 1. Wait until players are physiologically attentive to partners before coaching them to move apart.

2. Players can actually lower their voices as they put distance between them; conversations can be held in murmur from as far away as forty feet.

3. The sidecoaching phrase **Close your eyes!** opens players to the fact that they are not lipreading. The whole body from head to foot is involved with the spoken word.

4. Have players think of words as sound which they shape or design into word patterns.

5. Move among players so you can sidecoach the several conversations simultaneously.

6. It is recommended that the teacher try this one out as a player with friends to get an experience of the game beforehand.

Part 1:
Vowels!
Feel, touch the vowels!
Let the vowels touch you!
Consonants!
Talk normally!
See, feel, focus on the consonants!

Part 2:
Move back from each other!
Vowels! . . . Consonants!
Speak more softly than before!
Move as far back as possible!

Part 3:
Move in closer!
Speak more softly yet!
Vowels! . . . Consonants!
Close your eyes!
Speak as quietly as possible!
Move into your first positions!

Did you feel as though you were touching the words you spoke?
Did you communicate with your partner the whole time?

— BUILDING A STORY ——————————————

Purpose: To listen with full awareness and understanding to the words of a story.

Focus: On full physical attention to the words of a story.

Description: Large group sits in a circle. Sidecoach chooses one player to begin telling a story. The story can be known or made up. At any moment in the story, the sidecoach points at random to a player who must immediately pick up where the last player left off, even if in the middle of a word. Players are not to repeat the last word of the previous storyteller.

Example: First player, "The wind blew . . ." Second player, "the hat off his head."

Notes: 1. To keep players at high energy levels and totally involved with the process, the sidecoach must catch them off balance, in the middle of a thought or sentence.

2. Pre-planning what to say fragments and alienates players. Point to the player least expecting it. Spontaneity results only when players stay with the moment the story is being told.

3. Too many players starting with "and" indicates that the sidecoach is not catching players off guard.

4. Additional sidecoaching: Coach players to tell their part of the story in **Verrry slooooooow motionnn.** Then have them return to normal speed.

5. Let the player who has difficulty in finding words speak no more than a few words at a time at first, but surprise that player by returning to him or her again and again for a few words until the fear of failing is dissipated.

6. For review, we suggest that a tape recording be made of players' stories.

7. This game lends itself well to many variations such as the following.

Variation: When players become familiar with this game, have them attempt to build sentences one word at a time, one word per player.

Keep the story going!
Stay with the word!
Don't plan ahead!
Aim for one story, one voice!
Keep the word in the space!
Share your voice!

Were players caught up in the idea of where the story should go?
Or did they stay with the words as the story evolved?
Did it become as one story told by one voice?
Did the story keep building?
Which part of the story did you like best? Why?
Did the story end as it should have?
What other endings are possible?

—— BUILDING A STORY: STOP MID-WORD ——

Purpose: To increase acuteness in listening to and telling a story.

Focus: On continuing a story from the middle of a word.

Description: Five to fifteen players play this game in turn around a circle. First player starts the story and, when he/she wishes, stops in the middle of a word. Next player must continue the story by finishing the previous player's unfinished word and going on. Once the group becomes comfortable with the game, the next player may be pointed to at random rather than taking turns around the circle.

Note: This game can be played by two players with ease and enjoyment.

Don't plan ahead!
Aim for one story, one voice!
Share your voice!

Were players able to continue the story from the middle of a word? Did completed words continue the story?

—— BUILDING A STORY: READING ——

Purpose: To follow a story attentively with both ears and eyes.

Focus: On staying with the words being read aloud.

Description: Teams of equally skilled readers or regular reading groups. Each team reads the same selection at the same time. Sidecoach taps a player to start reading aloud. All players must follow along silently word for word because sidecoach will switch the reading aloud from player to player at random. New reader called may not repeat the last word spoken by the previous reader or skip any words in the text.

Note: To keep the game challenging and fun for all, changes from player to player should be called mid-sentence.

Share your voice!
Keep your eye on the word!

Did you notice any words repeated or skipped?

— Relating an Incident Adding Color —

Purpose: To add dimensions to *Where*, both in perceiving and describing.

Focus: On seeing an incident in full color as it is being told.

Description: Two players. A tells B a simple story (an incident limited to five or six sentences). B then retells the same story, adding as much color as possible.

Example: A narrates: "I walked down the street and saw an accident between a car and a truck in front of the school building . . ." B retells: "I was walking cheerfully down the grey street and saw an accident between a green car and a brown truck on the icy street in front of the red brick school . . ."

Notes: 1. The purpose of the game is for the listener to see the incident in full color at the moment of listening to it.

2. Other qualities may be substituted for color (texture, odor, sounds, shapes), as may adverbs and adjectives.

3. Even if they have no experience of world literature, students may be interested in the way this game reflects the growth of the oral tradition. In many cultures, history is whatever is remembered and repeated from generation to generation. Sometimes stories have been written down and become great works of literature. Homer's *Iliad* and *Odyssey* are based on oral traditions as are *The Song of Roland* and American Indian legends.

See the other player!
Don't wait to add color!
See the color as you hear the story!
Talk directly to one another!
Share your voice!

Players, did you add as much color as possible?
Did you change the story in any other way or did you stick to what your partner said?
Audience, do you agree with players?

Chapter 16:
STORYTELLING
AND STORY THEATER

Building Larger Scenes through Theater Games

Storytelling and story theater are overlapping forms of performance art which can be successfully used to tell longer stories. They both use narration (and thus go back to the earliest history of dramatic presentation).

Storytelling

With a storyteller supplying narration, students can perform longer dramatic pieces. The storyteller relates the story to the players as they stand in the playing area and they follow his or her direction. (It is wise to assign the selection or composition of the story to be used a week in advance. That way, pictures of characters and sets can be drawn, costumes and props can be chosen. The drawings, in particular, will stimulate the storyteller in organizing the material.)

Unless the group is unusually large, one storyteller per session is usually sufficient. The story should not take more than half an hour with younger children and can often take much less time. The storyteller either picks out a story or makes one up. (Oftentimes children narrate and play a story derived from BUILDING A STORY, above.)

(To ensure players are attentive to the storyteller it is useful to play FOLLOW THE FOLLOWER as a warm-up.)

Once the story is chosen and prepared, the storyteller does the casting and shows the drawings to the cast. Using any of the Where games as lead-ins, let the storyteller set up the *Where* in the playing space and have the individual players make themselves familiar with the setting.

When ready to start, the storyteller takes a place at the side of the playing area and begins to read or recite. The players dramatize the story as it is told. Pieces that work well can be presented to an audience.

This game is of special value to the aspiring director as young as six to eight because it gives the storyteller the total view of theater performance and an understanding

☐ *Storytelling requires considerable concentration and cooperation.*

☐ *Storytelling is also valuable for older children and adults. It is a means by which the world of fine literature can be given life in the classroom. (A listing of resource materials for storytelling and other theater games can be found in the bibliography.)*

☐ *It is of vital importance, as noted below, that the storyteller paraphrase the dialogue of the characters. This may be difficult to impart at first, but constant hammering at the point will eventually make storytelling classes much more exciting.*

of the problems of integrating the different elements into a scene. Like directors, storytellers soon discover that every performer must be dealt with as a special case. During a storytelling of "Jack and the Beanstalk," the giant was a boy of six who sat by most passively while Jack stole all his things. The storyteller, wishing to get some emotional response out of the giant, said, "The giant was very angry when he woke up and found his eggs gone." The little boy on stage merely opened his eyes wider and looked blandly about. This did not satisfy the storyteller, so she tried again. "And the giant was very angry, and he jumped up and down." Our giant tried to do this but without pleasing the narrator, for she continued, "The giant was real angry. He had never been so mad before, and he jumped and hollered and said all kinds of rude things."

Then, to the satisfaction of all present, the six-year-old giant roared out, "Darn it all, who stole my eggs!?"

□ *Sometimes, after a storytelling session, it is valuable to pick out a few points to work on and choose some specific exercises for the actors to do.*

□ *The storyteller becomes a guide, relieving the players of concern as to where the story is going.*

STORYTELLING

Purpose: To integrate theater and narrative.

Focus: On the story.

Description: The storyteller may be a member of the group or someone from outside. (The teacher may be storyteller the first time or two but should ultimately act as director, sitting close to the storyteller to aid in keeping the whole cast and backstage crew working together.) The storyteller comes to class with a narrative or poem rehearsed. He or she should have a list of the characters in the story and the text should be marked for pauses where major stage action will be necessary. The storyteller assigns the roles of the characters in the story or poem to players in the class. A technical crew (to control lights and/or set props and furniture) is also selected. (If the storyteller is a member of the class, preparation should not take long. But if the storyteller is an outsider let the teacher assign roles.) If pictures or background biographies of the characters have been prepared by the storyteller, they are shown or read to the cast and crew.

The storyteller then relates the story to the actors onstage and they enact it. To avoid having the players merely stand in place and parrot the storyteller, make sure the players are not given set lines or told exactly what to do. For example, the actors have little leeway if the storyteller reads, "Then the mother said, 'I love you, Jack,' and the little boy hugged her." It is better to narrate, "Then the mother told the little boy she loved him and he was happy again."

Notes: 1. See comments in paragraph 2, above. It may be difficult at first for the storyteller to give the actors room to invent their own dialogue and actions. But once the point has been made clear storytelling will be much more exciting. See the examples below.

2. *Commedia dell'arte* is an Italian form of comedy which greatly influenced Molière. It does not include a storyteller but does have "stock" characters (Scapino, Pantalone, Colombine, etc.) played by actors who improvise, scene by scene, whole plays based on a prearranged outline of a plot. The great twentieth-century dramatist Pirandello was also interested in this form.

3. See also such related games as CHORAL READING.

Follow the follower!
See the word!

Audience, what parts of the story did you like best?
Which seemed most real? Why?
Did the characters do what you expected them to do?
Players, when did you feel closest to the characters?
Storyteller, did the actors surprise you by saying or doing things you hadn't imagined?
Players, would you like changes in the story? Where?
Audience, do you agree with the plot changes the players are recommending?
How would you rewrite the story?

Story Theater

Story theater incorporates the storyteller's narration into dramatic scenes. It is a simple and effective way to present myths, legends, and fairy tales without props, elaborate scenery, or extensive technical knowledge, and without sacrificing true theater values. The players use body movement and space objects to convey the story. Very minimal sets and props (or none at all) are used. Story theater, therefore, is ideally suited to the classroom.

In performance, players are at once the characters and the storytellers, working in simple open space, creating settings with vocal sound effects and minimal lighting, with only an occasional need for blocks or ramps to give shape to a set. In story theater, the sense of time and space is effected through the narration and dialogue of the performers.

☐ *Paul Sills writes in* Story Theater, *"All properties in Story Theater are found or made in space; what they are is shown to the audience by the way the player shapes and handles the space."*

A story theater performance looks like this: At the start of "Jack and the Beanstalk," a player comes onstage and speaks directly to the audience.

JACK: Once upon a time there lived a boy by the name of Jack.
(As player is talking, he becomes the character JACK. Continuing narration)
One day Jack was walking about looking for his cow, Bessie.
(JACK continues to move about the playing area, establishing for the audience where he is. RELAY WHERE, WHERE GAME WITH PROPS, or SHOWING WHERE WITHOUT OBJECTS and other Where games are useful rehearsal tools for this moment)

☐ *Sills also says, "The players show the scene as they show the props, by the way they respond to the dark wood or glittering palace of the story, brushing branches aside as if the space took this form, or opening curtains, carrying space burdens, etc. . . . One of the particular pleasures of Story Theater is when the invisible becomes visible."*

JACK: *(Continuing narration in character)*
Jack continues to search all over for Bessie.

MOTHER: *(Enters and begins narration to the audience players)* Jack's mother was looking for her boy, as she had something very important to tell him.
(Begins looking about for JACK)

BESSIE: *(While the above is going on, BESSIE enters and saunters about the playing area)* Moo. Moo.

MOTHER: *(Finding JACK)* Jack, we have to sell Bessie.

(BESSIE sidles up to JACK, who scratches her ear)

JACK: Why must we do that, Mother?

MOTHER: We are very poor, son, and Bessie has stopped giving milk, and without milk to sell, we have no way of earning any money.

JACK: But Mother, how can we sell Bessie?

(JACK makes the bare stage a farm, by taking hay from a space-substance haystack and feeding a cow. Changes in the Where *are easily brought about through the players' narration. For example:)*

JACK: *(Narrating and physicalizing)* So Jack, leading Bessie, slowly headed down the road toward the County Fair, when suddenly . . .

BEAN SELLER: *(Narrating)* He was greeted by a funny-looking old man who said to him . . .
(Dialogue) Well, young man, where are you off to, with that fine cow?

JACK: I'm going to the Fair to sell our cow.

The combination of narration and dialogue continues on to the end of the story.

As a foundation for both STORYTELLING and story theater, tell stories to your group as part of their theater training. Let the children themselves tell stories. Stories can be used as a part of regular workshop theater games and can eventually lead to group selection of stories for performance.

The following steps will lead to a full-length scene.

A. Find a story for development.

B. Familiarize the class with the story. Read it aloud. Have students take turns reading it. Play GIVE & TAKE FOR READING; use BUILDING A STORY to retell the story. Divide the group up in pairs and have players tell one another the story using MIRROR SPEECH or VOWELS &

☐ *If players suggest additions to or changes in the story, be flexible. Alterations are sometimes improvements.*

SONANTS.

Explore the *Where*. What do players see in the story? players relate the story to one another using RELAT-
N INCIDENT ADDING COLOR and VERBALIZING THE
E. As players see each aspect of the *Where* in all the
of the story, inventory all the things players see.
se of the *Where* will become very rich.

st the story. This can be done by the leader alone
o   -casting. To accommodate a large group, you may
n   o two or three stories. Select technical and off-
st   rs to be in charge of vocal sound effects (see
Ch   EADING and SOUNDTRACK).

ll players help develop a skeleton of the play.
The   ng will serve as an example:

The   Little Pigs (Skeleton)

1. A   r Mother Pig sends her three children out into the world to seek their fortunes.
2. The first little pig is given straw by a peasant and builds a straw house.
3. A wolf comes, blows down the straw house, and chases the little pig away. (The first and second pigs are, of course, eaten in some versions.)
4. The second little pig receives sticks from a woodcutter and builds a house of sticks.
5. The wolf comes, blows down the stick house, and chases the second little pig away.
6. The third (and cleverest) little pig gets bricks from a mason and builds a house of bricks.
7. The wolf comes and tries to blow down the house. When he fails, he tries other tricks to get in, but is still unsuccessful. He decides to try sliding down the chimney.
8. The third little pig builds a big fire in the fireplace to keep out the wolf.
9. The chimney is too hot for the wolf, so, giving up, he goes away. (In many versions, the wolf comes to his end in a pot on the third pig's stove.)
10. The third pig fetches the mother (and the remaining brothers or sisters), and they live happily ever after in the brick house.

F. You may set the script at this point or not. The narration each player will speak on his or her own character's behalf will (for the most part) be found in the text of the story. Dialogue also is usually in the text, but *do* leave out all the "She said"s. (Notice that it is a rare fairy tale that requires a particular line to be spoken. Traditionally, for example, the giant of "Jack and the Beanstalk" says "Fee-fi-fo-fum . . .," but no specific dialogue is recorded for Jack or his mother.)

G. Begin work on playing the story. Ask players:
—What vocal sound effects can be used?
—Will any costume parts be necessary?
—Can players become physical objects, trees, houses, flowers, etc.?

Additional stories particularly suitable for story theater include the following from Grimm, Aesop, Lear, Andersen, and others. (See Bibliography for sources.)

> "The Three Bears"
> "The Three Billy Goats Gruff"
> "Little Red Riding Hood"
> "Rumplestiltskin"
> "Rapunzel"
> "The Fox and the Grapes"
> "The Owl and the Pussycat"
> "The Ugly Duckling"

Students should also have the freedom to find their own material.

Slightly more complex folk legends can also be used as a basis for scenes. Here is a skeleton for the African folktale "The King's Drum," with a few suggested possibilities for action:

The King's Drum (Skeleton)

1. The King called a meeting of all his subjects. It took them weeks to get there.
2. The King said they must find a way to gather more quickly.
3. Anansi the spider, the King's counsellor, suggested that a royal drum be built to signal meetings.
4. Going to the faraway forest, the animals organized themselves into groups to build the drum. But the

☐ *The King's subjects, we will learn, are the animals. Have each student select an animal to play and discover the cause of his or her delay.*

☐ *Let students select the groups they want to work in and the kind of work they will do: tree cutting, hollowing, decorating the drum.*

monkey did no work. Instead he went looking for berries, singing a song. Anansi saw him but said nothing.

5. When the drum was finished, the King announced a welcoming ceremony at the palace.

6. But the distance the drum had to come was many miles and the drum was large and heavy. No one wanted to carry it. The leopard urged that the lion do the honors, the lion offered the job to the antelope, the antelope recommended the elephant, and so on.

7. Anansi suggested that the drum be carried by the laziest animal. Nobody spoke up, but, one by one, the animals all turned to look at the monkey.

8. The monkey refused firmly.

9. The porcupine and several other animals pointed out that the monkey's name had not been mentioned.

10. Anansi the spider said that the monkey himself had volunteered the information, proving that he was the laziest.

11. When the King's drum was brought to the palace for the welcoming ceremony, it was the monkey who carried it.

□ *What song might the monkey and/or the working animals sing?*

□ *Split focus here: working animals, Anansi, and the monkey are all on stage.*

□ *Use slow motion at this moment. It builds suspense and makes the situation seem funnier.*

□ *There should be singing again here; let the animals begin the ceremony.*

Chapter 17:
PLAYMAKING FOR
AUDIENCE INVOLVEMENT

Learning an appreciation of the role of the audience must become a part of theater training. Too often the audience is regarded either as a cluster of peeping toms merely to be tolerated or as a many-headed monster sitting in judgment. In fact the audience should be the most revered member of the theater. Without an audience there is no theater.

All of the theater-game work to this point has been geared to playing with fellow players serving as an audience. This is intrinsic to theater-game training. It brings to fruition the whole creative process of theater. It helps establish that the audience must be involved in the process. The audience at a play is the last spoke which completes the wheel. No one should take advantage of an audience for self-glorification or exhibitionistic reasons. If this is done, everything you and your players have worked for will be dissipated. On the other hand, if the whole concept of sharing with the audience is understood, players will give exciting performances.

□ *The phrase "Forget the audience" is used by many directors as a means of helping the student actor to relax on stage. But this attitude is impossible to achieve. The actor must no more forget the audience than lines, props, or fellow players.*

Playing House

Children can discover the nature of onstage reality for themselves. After a group of six- and seven-year-olds experienced the fun of playing house on stage, the following discussion took place.

"Were you playing house or doing a play"?

"We were doing a play."

"What is the difference between playing house in your backyard and playing house here?"

"You have a stage here."

"Do you call it playing house here?"

"No. You call it a play."

"What else do you have here besides a stage?"

"An audience."

"Why does an audience come to see a play?"

"They like to . . . it's fun."

□ *Improvising a situation on stage has, like each of the games, its own kind of organization.*

"Did you make the playing house you just did fun for an audience?"

"No."

"Why not?"

"We didn't share our voices and didn't make it more interesting for them."

"What could you do to make it more interesting?"

"We could be naughty or all want to watch TV at the same time or something." (Note that, in time, children do learn that conflict isn't the only way to make stage activity interesting. Many adults share the same misconception.)

"I'd like to ask you again. Were you playing house just now or were you doing a play about a house?"

"We were playing house."

"Do you think you could go back on stage and do a play about a family in a house? Instead of playing house the way you do at home, could you show us where you are and who you are and what you are doing there?"

"Yes."

The scene was done again, retaining all the fun of the first playing while adding the players' real effort to "make it more interesting for the audience." The spontaneity and charm of the backyard playing was retained along with the added reality achieved in trying to share their experience with the audience. The child, too, can learn not to pretend but to make action real. A group of eight- to eleven-year-olds were questioned as to why they needed to make things real for the audience and not pretend. "If you pretend, it isn't real, and the audience can't see."

☐ *Children can learn the theater magic of "pulling a rabbit out of a hat."*

Understanding the Audience

In workshops with younger children, moving from subjective dramatic play into objective stage reality goes more slowly than with older students. In most cases, the child players are not yet mature enough to cope with anything more than the briefest evaluation period and there is a greater dependency upon the teacher — a dependency that cannot be broken too abruptly.

By separating dramatic play from, and then bringing it to, the theater experience, children can learn to differentiate between pretend (illusion) and their own everyday

☐ *All student actors, young and old alike, must learn that the stage is the stage and not an extension of life. It has its own life and the players agree to it, then play it, and then go on to something else.*

worlds. This separation is not implicit in dramatic play. Dramatic play and real life are often confused by the young and by many adults as well.

Introduce the idea of an audience to students by engaging them in conversation.

"Do you enjoy reading or having stories read to you?"

"Yes."

"What do you do while your mother is reading you a story?"

"We listen . . . we hear it."

"What do you hear?"

"You hear the story."

"Just what do you mean you 'hear the story?' Just what do you hear?"

"You hear what's happening in the story."

"Let's suppose your mother was reading you the story, 'The Three Bears.' What do you hear in that story?"

"You hear about the bears and the porridge."

"How do you know you're hearing about the three bears?"

"Because the words tell you you are."

"Now comes the important part: How do you know what the words tell you?"

"You can see."

"What do you see? The words?"

"No!" With much laughter, they tell you, "You see the three bears, of course!"

Continue the discussion about "seeing the words." Then tell them a story: "Once upon a time, there was a little boy and a little girl and they lived in a bright yellow house on top of a green hill. Every morning a little pink cloud floated by the house . . . ." (etc.) Ask the children what they saw. Keep it a group discussion. Have them describe the color they visualized for the girl's dress, what kind of a roof the little house had, etc. Keep up with this discussion as long as the interest level is high, then go on to the next point.

"What is the first thing your mother does when she is going to read you a story?"

"She comes into my bedroom . . . she sits down . . . she says, 'For five minutes, dear' . . ."

"Then what does she do?"

"She reads the story."

"How does she do that?"

"She reads it from the book!" By now the young players are certain that they have a "silly" teacher who doesn't know the simplest things.

"Now think hard. What is the first thing she does before she starts reading, after she has sat down, after she has come into the bedroom?"

"She opens the book!"

"Of course! She opens the book! Would it be possible to read the story if your mother didn't open the book?"

"Of course not."

"In theater, too, we have a story. And, we too must open the book before we begin. Only, on stage, we open the curtain. Or we turn on all the lights. Or we simply call out the word, 'Curtain!' How does the story usually begin?"

"Once upon a time, there was . . . ."

"You mean it starts in a place, somewhere?"

"Yes."

"Are there usually people in the story?"

"Yes, people and animals."

"The people in the story of Goldilocks and the Three Bears are called characters when we take them on stage. Now, just as your mother opens the book and begins with 'Once upon a time. . . .' we are going to show the bears and the house. Instead of seeing them in your head as when you are read to, you are going to see them on stage.

"When your mother reads you a story, does she whisper so you cannot hear her? Does she read from another room in the house?"

"Of course not! She reads the story so that we can hear it."

"Because if you couldn't hear it, you couldn't enjoy it. Right?

"The theater has people who are just like you when you're listening to your mother. The theater has an audience. They are our guests. The audience wants to enjoy the story they are seeing and hearing on the stage. And, just as your mother shares with you the 'once upon a time' and the characters (*Who*) in the book and what is happening to them (*What*), so, the actors must share the story they are playing on stage with the audience. And show them everything: where they are, who they are, and what they are doing.

"Does the audience sit and only listen the way you do

when you hear a story?"

"No, an audience looks. It's like watching TV..."

"Yes, an audience looks at what you are doing and sees the characters move around and do things and talk to each other. So the way to help the audience enjoy themselves is to show them as much as you can and to share with them everything you do on our playing area here."

Remember, it will take time before players become comfortable with an audience. The following games will help them become more aware of the audience.

□ *The foregoing kind of discussion gives the teacher an opportunity to bring the idea behind sidecoaching phrases like* **Share!** *and* **Show! Don't tell!** *into the workshop. However, immediate results will not be achieved.*

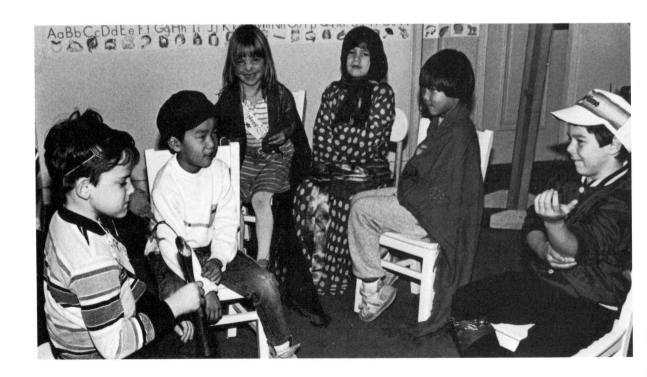

— EYE CONTACT —————————————

Purpose: To make players *see* one another.

Focus: On making direct eye contact with other players and directing sight to the prop or stage area to which reference is made.

Description: Two or more players. *Who*, *What*, and *Where* are agreed upon.

Example: Mary enters the room to visit John. John: "Hello, Mary" (eye contact to Mary). "Won't you come into the room?" (eye contact to room). Mary: "Hello, John" (eye contact to John). "Here's the book I said I'd bring" (eye contact directly to book). "Do you want it?" (eye contact to John).

Variation: To help actors "project" have them focus on making contact with every member of the audience.

Note: To get the heightened energy or extra focus, suggest that players' eyes take a close-up as a camera does. Doing this at the moment of eye contact is good even though it may be exaggerated. In time actors will learn to integrate eye contact subtly with all their work.

See!
Sell!
Teach!

Did they solve the problem?
Was extra focus (energy) given at the time of eye contact?

— PITCHMAN —————————————

Purpose: To break down barriers between players and audience.

Focus: On communicating with the audience.

Description: Single player. The player must sell or demonstrate something. After going through a speech once, player is asked to repeat it again, but this time to *pitch* it to the audience, that is, to make direct visual contact with the members of the audience.

Notes: 1. See notes to GIBBERISH: SELLING.

2. The audience members will recognize that a pitchman must be closely involved with them in order to communicate and will find themselves responding more emotionally.

3. Students who have any experience with consumer education will be particularly interested in this game. How do we respond to "hard sell" salesmanship? Might a "cooler" approach make the product being sold seem more attractive? What ads work best?

Pitch to us!
Heighten!
Stronger!

What was the difference between the two speeches?
Why did the pitching make the player come to life?

—— DEAF AUDIENCE ——————————————

Purpose: To develop physical communication.

Focus: On communicating a scene to a deaf audience.

Description: Two or more players. *Who, Where,* and *What* agreed upon. Members of the audience plug up their ears while watching the scene. Players are to go through scene as they normally would, using both dialogue and action.

Variation: Have audience close eyes instead of plugging ears.

Notes: 1. As members of the audience, players realize the necessity of showing, not telling.

2. The lifelessness of a scene in which actors merely talk instead of playing becomes evident to the most resistant.

3. If actors are aware that some members of the audience are stopping up their ears while others are closing their eyes they will — by trying to reach both groups — sense the importance of full-body communication.

Communicate!
Don't tell; do!
Show us!

Was the scene lively?
Did you know what was going on even though you could not hear the actors?

— Exits & Entrances —————————————

Purpose: To develop active response to stage life.

Focus: On making exits and entrances to get full involvement with fellow players.

Description: Teams of four, five, or six players agree on *Where*, *Who*, and *What*. Each player makes as many exits and entrances as possible with *Where*, *Who*, and *What*, but each exit or entrance must be so framed that onstage players are fully involved with the player's entrance or exit. If players barge in or slip out without the full involvement of fellow players, audience players are free to call out: "Come back!" or "Go back! You didn't make it!" There are many exciting and challenging ways to meet an audience!

Notes: 1. There must be heightened focus on a player's entrance or exit, if only for a fleeting moment. It is sharpness in framing such details that gives the stage clarity and brilliance.

2. Devices such as shouting, stomping feet, jumping up and down, etc. may bring attention to the oncoming player but not the involvement with *Where*, *Who*, and *What* which is needed for the playing (process) to continue. However, if onstage players give attention and become involved in player's exit or entrance, no action is barred, no matter how fanciful it may be. Therefore, if exit or entrance involves *Where*, *Who*, and *What*, players may crawl out, dance in, fly out again, or enter with a quiet "hello."

3. Exits & Entrances should make clear the difference between getting attention (an isolated player) and becoming involved (part of the whole).

4. Homework: Ask players to take note when entering a room how often people (themselves included) are satisfied when they receive passing attention rather than involvement or engagement.

Keep onstage movement!
Don't plan your exits!
Watch for the moment!
Stay with the activity!
Play the game!
Let exits (entrances) come through **Where, Who,** *and* **What!**

Which exits and entrances truly had full involvement and which were only trying to get attention? Players, do you agree?

Chapter 18:
PUBLIC PERFORMANCE

Public performances, when children are ready, will raise their level of understanding and sharpen their skills. However, do not take this step prematurely. Be certain that players have integrated their workshop training and will share their play with an audience of outsiders. Even children in primary grades can learn to handle the tools of the theater with sensitivity, working with you and their fellow players to perform in public showings.

From time to time open up a regular classroom workshop to outside guests as an informal audience. This open workshop performance is particularly recommended for younger children. If focus is maintained by players during your regular workshops, it will be easier to maintain playing the same type of games in front of their families and friends.

For an almost instant performance piece for pageants, recitals, etc., try having your children play a traditional singing game such as PRINCESS THORN ROSA or ISABELLA. These even allow for simple costume pieces and are filled with dramatic elements which delight both players and audiences.

Once, in a play where a doll shop was an important setting, six-year-olds were used as dolls. Some research was done on the characters by the young actors. A couple of dolls were brought to class and the children found that they moved stiffly at the joints. In movement class, they worked on solving the problem of doing everything as dolls. They played "doll shop" for weeks prior to rehearsing with the full cast of older children (who were eleven to fifteen). By the time the young children cast as dolls were brought to rehearsals, they seemed like veteran actors. The only thing they had to do was to work with the older players.

Stands were built for the dolls, on which the children could sit during performance. They were told that if a pin was sticking them from their costume, they should remove it. They could brush their hair out of their eyes, sneeze if necessary, or cough. There was just one focus: they were to move as dolls no matter what happened.

Some of the most charming moments of the show thus

☐ *Players must understand that the audience is "part of the game" and not merely exhibit themselves.*

☐ *Viewing theater-game problem solving is most engaging for an audience. Theater games have been performed by professional acting companies in Chicago, Los Angeles, New York, and other theater centers for decades.*

occurred when they were least expected — when a nose had to be scratched or when a hat fell off. Many adults were amazed at the relaxed quality of the children, at their lack of affectation and their doll-like movements. They were surprised at the "acting" of these "babies."

After one performance, the little talking doll (six years old) was besieged by children from the audience. Even a few adults clustered around her, crooning: "Isn't she darling! Isn't she the little actress!" The fuss would have been enough to turn the head of many an older person, but the little girl merely thanked the group and, turning to another player, asked, "Did you think my focus was complete?"

In time the theater-game approach to teaching and learning drama in the classroom will help players become so physically attuned to the freedoms and limitations of the theater and their responsibility to an audience that there will never be any need for a typical "ignore the audience" speech before curtain.

Developing the Scripted Play

The following notes are intended for the teacher who wants to perform a scripted play. Whether the play you choose to perform is one you and your group created from stories and poems in theater-game workshops or one already scripted by others, your children will clamor to take copies home and "learn their lines." However, the theater-game approach to theater training calls for total integration of body and mind, words and actions. Therefore, we recommend strongly that scripts stay in the classroom so that lines are learned in context.

Choosing the Play

It is difficult to set down a blueprint for choosing a play. However, there are a few specific questions which the teacher should address before making a final decision:
   1. Who will my audience be?
   2. How skillful are my actors?
   3. Do I have a technical staff that can handle the effects the play needs?
   4. Is it a play *I* can handle?

   5. Will the play respond to my work on it?
   6. Is the play worth doing?
   7. Is it in good taste?
   8. Will it give a fresh experience, provoke individual thought and thereby insight for the audience?
   9. Is the play theatrical?
 10. Will it be a creative experience for all?
 11. Will it be fun to do? Will it play?

Throughout rehearsal periods, constantly question:

   1. How can the playwright's intent be clarified?
   2. Are performers' individual mannerisms getting in the way?
   3. Should the scene be heightened visually with more purposeful blocking and business, unusual props or effects?
   4. Are crowd or party scenes handled ineffectively?
   5. Should we play more games?

A Timetable for Rehearsals

The overall rehearsal schedule can be broken down into three periods. The first period is for laying the groundwork. The second period is for developing the theme of the piece and the third period is for polishing.

The theme of a piece is the moving thread that weaves itself into every small section — every "beat" of the play or scene. It shows itself within the simplest gesture of the player and in the last bits of trim on a costume. Sometimes, watching and listening, it is a single word or phrase that sparks understanding in us; sometimes it is simply a nonverbal feeling that develops slowly. The director may find the theme before rehearsals begin, or well into rehearsals. The rehearsal period should be structured as follows:

☐ *The director should think of theme as the thread that links all the parts of a production together.*

☐ *Don't, in desperation, impose a theme upon the play. Randomness could be a theme.*

The First Rehearsal Period

Sit-Down Readings
   A. Director reads the script aloud (optional).
   B. Parts are given out.
   C. All read their lines aloud. Pronunciation and typographical errors are cleaned up. (Don't be afraid to sidecoach during readings.)
   D. Read again using VOWELS AND CONSONANTS.
   E. Read again using SPELLING.
   F. Read again coaching **Slow motion!** to underscore critical moments in the text.
   G. Read again straight through without stopping.

After two or three sit-down readings like those outlined, the group should be relaxed, familiar with the script and each other, and in a pleasant, anticipatory mood. Everyone enters the spirit of playing, freed of tensions.

□ *When players realize that learning the lines, interpreting the script, forming the characters, etc., are not required at the beginning, a great sense of release will be evident.*

Walk-Through Rehearsals
Set doors, stairs, etc., keeping settings general. If you are working on a costume play, give some suggestions to players about what they will be wearing, whether it be hoop skirt or stiff collar. Sidecoach during walk-throughs when necessary: **Share the stage picture! Share your voice! Vowels! Slooow motionnn!** Out of the onstage problems that begin to emerge will come the theater games to be played in your next workshop. While it may be true that your selection of a game is based on the special needs of one or two actors, all will benefit.

□ *What is called interpretation begins to emerge in a holistic approach to rehearsal, out of the merging of the work done by director, players, and playwright.*

Stage Movement (Blocking)
Blocking is essentially the choreography of stage movement. As simple as that may sound, moving actors about during a play often can be quite hazardous. The director cannot be in full control of the places actors stand or how they get on or off the stage. Blocking should facilitate movement, emphasize and heighten thought and action, strengthen relationships, and underline conflicts. As long as the actor is constantly directed in the mechanics of stage movement and does not understand that stage movement can only grow out of involvement and interrelating, the actor can at best only remember the conventions and will therefore be unable to move naturally.

□ *Blocking is the integration of the stage picture, a moving composition.*

Players with many months of workshop training behind them will be able to translate any directions given by playwright and director into necessary stage action. Playing STAGE PICTURE as a warm-up to rehearsals at this point in the production is very useful.

Where (The Set)

It is essential for players to get inside the set (the playing field) and not just pass through it. In this part of the rehearsal period, use Gibberish and Where games to assist players in making contact with their stage environment.

GIVE AND TAKE WARM-UP is also very useful during rehearsals to assist players in hearing and listening to their fellow players.

☐ *While it is sometimes necessary for a stage direction to be given to the actor, blocking must become an organic response to stage life. The following dialogue was with a ten-year-old player:*
> *"Why did you go upstage just then?"*
> *"Because you told me to."*
> *"Isn't that mechanical?"*
> *"Yes."*
> *"Why were you directed to go upstage?"*
> *"I went upstage so Tom could enter."*
> *"Why couldn't you wait for him where you were?"*
> *"I wasn't part of the scene going on at the moment."*
> *"How can you stand out of the scene and still be part of the stage picture?"*
> *"I'll put my focus on listening for Tom to come in."*

The Second Rehearsal Period

The Relaxed Rehearsal

When lines have been learned, the relaxed rehearsal gives perspective to players. Players lie on the floor with eyes shut and breathe with strong emphasis on exhalation. Walk among them, lifting a foot or a hand to make sure that muscular relaxation and release are complete. Players then go through the lines of the script with eyes closed continuing to focus on visualizing the stage, the other actors, and themselves in the scene. Quietly remind actors not to mouth others' words but to hear them, to keep focus on seeing the stage with eyes closed. If properly handled and prepared for, this time will be enjoyable for all. The onstage work will be heightened and the last vestiges of anxiety will eventually disappear.

General Improvisation around the Play

When it becomes necessary to provoke the players beyond the lines of the script and to sharpen relationships, general improvisation is most helpful. General improvisations will seem to have no direct relation to the written play. They are used to give players insight into the characters they are playing, into "seeing the words" and achieving a focus for the scene. SEEING THE WORD is useful for general improvisation around a play as are most Where and Who games.

Nonstop Run-Throughs

The nonstop run-through is especially valuable to the director with a limited amount of rehearsal time. It is, simply, a complete run-through of the play without stops of any kind. Under no circumstances break in. Take notes and go over them with actors later.

Biographies

Toward the end of the second rehearsal period, ask players for biographies of their characters. This device occasionally brings some insights to a player who seems to be getting nowhere with a part. A biography is everything about the character being played: schooling, parents, grandparents, favorite foods, main ambitions, loves, hates, what entertains, how evenings are spent. Then add what brought the character to this immediate stage situation. Allow no discussion about the biographies. Simply accept them as they are and use them for reference material if and when the need arises. Written analysis should not be done until the player is settling into the character — not too early.

□ *A biography written by a fourteen-year-old girl playing in a fantasy stated that she and the villain had gone to school together as children and that she had loved him very much. While logically this would have been impossible in the social setting of the play, this emotional involvement gave her relationship with the villain much greater depth. The audience, of course, was never aware of this story.*

The Third Rehearsal Period

This is the polishing period. The jewel has been cut and evaluated and now must be put into its setting. It is best to schedule spot rehearsals in the third period, when the play has shape and flow. The spot rehearsal gives special time to working over a troublesome scene which has not resolved itself within regular rehearsals.

The Special Run-Through

There are no mistakes on stage as far as the audience is concerned, for they usually do not know the script or the action of the play. So a player need never let the audience know when something is amiss.

The special run-through puts the cast completely on its own. At a regularly scheduled run-through of the play (just prior to dress rehearsal) tell the cast that in the event of a break of any kind (laughter, lost lines, etc.) by one of the actors, all — the full cast — must cover up and keep the scene going. Failing to do so, all go back to the beginning of the act. If, for instance, a player breaks at the very end of the second act and no one has covered this, the director quietly calls, "Begin the second act, please!" and the actors must go back over the ground they have just covered.

After a few "begin agains" you will find the cast putting some well-deserved peer pressure upon the culprit who made the break. Remind everyone that all are equally responsible for keeping the play going and they must cover for fellow players in case of trouble. At the same time it gives a deeper sense of security to the player to know that no matter what happens on stage, and whatever crisis or danger arises, the group will come to assistance for the sake of the play.

□ *The special run-through is the fullest expression of the group experience at work. The individual players must be very disciplined, for they are now directly responsible to the group.*

The special run-through is very exciting for the players and keeps all of them on their toes, alerted for that moment when it may become necessary to cover up for a fellow player. After one or two rehearsals, the show will go on even if the very roof should fall in.

The Performance

The performance brings to its fruition the whole creative process of doing the play. During the show, stay away from the backstage area. Everything must be so well organized that it runs smoothly without you. The players will grow in stature during the performances if properly prepared. In particular, false and dishonest characterizations and relationships become apparent.

□ *The stage is the X-ray picture where every secret structure shows up. If the play is presented shabbily, if its "bones" are weak, this will be seen, just as a fracture shows up in an X-ray.*

Workshops and rehearsals may not produce fully seasoned players in their first show, but all will be well on their way.

If, toward the end of the run, actors decide to "cut up," remind them that their last performance is the audience's first. Enjoyment must come from the performing itself, not from silly tricks played on fellow players.

Chapter 19:
ROUNDING OUT THE CHILD ACTOR

What we are trying to make happen is the acceptance of the invisible as a premise for connection between players and audience, connection being the real communication.

Inner Action

The concept behind inner action can easily be made clear to children, but it is best not to introduce it until the children have had a good deal of improvisation and storytelling. Here is an example of how to handle the concept of inner action when the workshop group is ready.

Do you know what your mother is feeling when you come home from school? If you want to go out and play and you have to ask permission, can you tell if your mother is in a good mood?

The smallest child nods, remembering.

How can you tell?

"By the way she looks . . . the way she acts."

Would someone like to go up and be a mother who is in a pleasant mood? Although young children rarely work alone, it is occasionally an excellent experience for them. Choose one of the volunteers.

The young player chosen goes on stage and becomes the "cheerful mother." When he or she has finished, either discuss the presentation with the group or have others go up individually and work on this single problem. The student audience will pay close attention.

Now have the children sit quietly and think about their families.

Can you usually tell when someone in your home is worried?

"Yes."

Ask them to show us. When it is clear that the group understands that people tend to show what they feel, then explain the acting problem as follows:

You are going to play a what-are-you-thinking-about game. Each of you will go into the playing area by yourself; you are to be somewhere, waiting for someone. While you are waiting, you are thinking about something. When you are through thinking, we in the audience will see whether we can know what you were thinking about. You may be waiting for someone who is late. You may be alone in a strange neighborhood and slightly afraid. You may be waiting for someone who is going to take you to a wonderful party. Everyone will guess at the inside thought.

After individual thinking of each has been communicated to the audience, put all the children together in a waiting room of a train station, for example. Here, players are to work on thinking the same thing they thought about earlier when they were working alone. (If class size is too large, divide class, half as players, half as audience players, then reverse.)

When this work is presented so that children are able to understand it in terms of their own expeience, some interesting inner action will result. Encourage the children to play a game of seeing "how people feel inside" outside of class. They will enjoy watching family and friends and knowing what they are thinking about.

The games in the following two sections, "Stage Work" and "Contact," isolate several aspects of performance and help players enhance their skills. But the last two sections, "Conflict" and "Role Playing," contain cautionary notes on maintaining a distance between improvisation and real life.

Stage Work

— STAGE PICTURE ———————————

Purpose: To recognize that any part of you is all of you.

Focus: On group creation.

Description: Players move in and out and around each other. When you call out **Stage picture!** players must instantly *hold*. If some part of each and every individual is not visible to the audience, continue to sidecoach **Stage picture!** Players then instantaneously do whatever will make a part of them visible. Some get down on their knees, others raise their arms; elbows appear. Many interesting and random formations result.

Variations: 1. Continuous moving stage picture: group stays in constant movement, all players keeping visible at all times.

2. Players move in and out and around one another. Sidecoach calls one player by name. All other players follow this one player until **Hold!** is sidecoached. Repeat with other players.

3. Two teams, one observes. As each stage picture is frozen, audience team infers a *Who/Where/What* from the players' positions.

Stage picture!
Continue!
Stage picture!
Continue! . . .

Variation #1:
Stage picture!
Stage picture! . . .

Variation #2:
(Name one player): *Hold!*
(Name another player): *Hold!*

Variation #3:
Audience, how did you reach your conclusions?
Players, how does your sense of the stage picture match what the audience saw?

—— STAGE WHISPER WARM-UP ★ ——

Focus: On releasing throat muscles and pouring full-body energy into an audible stage whisper.

Description: All players seated with both feet on the ground. Players are to pant out loud, trying to open their throats as much as possible. As throat muscles relax, players are to add vocal sounds to the panting. When sidecoached, players repeat simple words and numbers or rhymes using a stage whisper. For example: "Two, four, six, eight! Who do we appreciate?"

Notes: 1. A stage whisper is not a true whisper, for it must be shared with an audience and, in a sense, is "acting out" a whisper. If done properly, the voice will be resonant.

   2. If a slight dizziness occurs, simply stop the exercise for a while.

Release throat muscles!
Try to get that open throat!
Add sound!
Two! Four! Six! Eight!
Push sound from the bottom of the feet on up and out!

Where did you feel the energy coming from for the stage whisper?

—— STAGE WHISPER ——

Purpose: To develop dramatic moments.

Focus: On stage whispering with full projection and open throat.

Description: Teams of two or more players agree on *Where, Who,* and *What* in which the players are forced to whisper to each other. For example: thieves in a closet, lovers quarreling in the theater. Just before beginning the scene, players might sit and pant for a few seconds in the playing area.

Notes: 1. As this exercise requires a great deal of physical energy, the released energy brings alive, amusing, exciting stage situations, instant vignettes. If focus is kept on the stage whisper, this exercise almost invariably produces a theatrical experience for the players.

   2. Calling out **One minute to go!** may heighten a team's effort in this exercise.

   3. Reminder: Whenever players, because of audience response, get caught up in interesting dialogue or humor developing in the event (scene), sidecoach players back to the focus: **Stage whisper!**

Open your throat!
Use your whole body!
Whisper from the bottom of your feet on up!
Not a whisper . . . a stage whisper!
Share your stage whisper with the audience!
Focus on stage whisper! Stage whisper!

Did players talk softly or did they use a stage whisper?
Players, did you let the focus work for you?
Audience, do you agree?

—Rocking the Boat/ Sharing the Stage Picture

Purpose: To teach players self-blocking

Focus: On the stage picture.

Description: Divide the class into two or three large teams. Each team agrees on a *Where, Who,* and *What* and chooses a familiar theater game. (The most likely are Who Am I? or Box Full of Hats.) Players are to think of the stage or playing area as a small boat or canoe at sea. Discuss what happens to a boat if all the passengers sit on one side. Ask players if there are times onstage when we want to "rock the boat." To the chosen theater game add the additional rule that when ***Rock the boat!*** is sidecoached, players are to unbalance the stage deliberately. When, on the other hand ***Share the stage picture!*** is coached, players are to balance the stage picture. All movement is to be integrated within *Where, Who,* and *What.*

Notes: 1. Sidecoached during any theater game, ***You're rocking the boat!*** or ***Share the stage picture!*** encourages self-blocking by giving every player the responsibility of the total stage picture.

2. These sidecoaching phrases should always be given to the full group rather than one individual player, for then all players must see themselves in physical relation to fellow players and act within the total stage picture.

Rock the boat!
(After a time:)
Don't rock the boat!
Share the stage picture!

Contact

We sometimes see plays where children stay in their own little areas — afraid to touch, look directly at, or listen to each other. Strong contacts between players, when a hand really holds another's arm or an eye looks into an eye, make productions more alive, more solid. An audience is able to sense when real contact has been made. Coach players on this throughout workshops.

CONTACT can heighten highly dramatic scenes. Here the actors cannot escape into dialogue and character, but must stand and be seen. This forces all players to make finer choices of stage movement.

☐ *Contact may be made either through direct physical touch, the passing of props, or eye focus.*

☐ *Take time out to do a scene from a play as a contact exercise.*

─ CONTACT ─────────────────────────────

Purpose: To force all players to rely directly on their inner resources. To give stage business variety. To help players see and be seen.

Focus: On making direct physical contact with each new thought or phrase of dialogue.

Description: Two or more players agree on *Where, Who,* and *What.* They improvise a scene. Each player is to make direct physical contact with a fellow player as each new thought or phrase is introduced. Contact should be limited to head, shoulders, arms, hands, legs, feet and back and, of course, be nonviolent. Each time a speaker begins, a direct physical contact must be made. Players are responsible for their own dialogue and contact. Nonverbal communications (nods, whistles, shrugs, etc.) are acceptable without contact. If contact cannot be made, there is to be no dialogue. (As a surprise to players, add more challenging rules as in sidecoaching for Parts 2 through 4.)

Notes: 1. Players resist contact out of fear of touching one another. This shows itself in irritation at having to find variety; in poking and pushing other players away; in trying to make contact through props; in using only the most casual, constricted contact (tapping on shoulders, etc.). Go back to earlier exercises emphasizing relationships, body movements, and space substance.

2. If players do not wait for the focus to work for them, they will fall into irrelevant ad-libbing, poke at each other instead of making contact, and invent useless activity. Use sidecoaching Parts 2, 3, and 4 to help players vary contact.

3. Suggest players attempt to make nonverbal contact with a family member or friend without letting the other know. Discuss the various responses players received.

Part 1:
Contact! (Whenever players speak without touching.)
Vary the contact!
Be quiet if you cannot make contact!
Use your full playing area!
Play the game!

Part 2:
No contact twice in the same part of the body!

Part 3:
No hands!
No contact with hands!

Part 4:
No contact with feet!

Was involvement between players greater because of contact? Was there variety in the contact? Did the contact come out of Who, *or was it done mechanically? Players, did you keep focus on making contacts or were you concerned with the activity and scene?*

Conflict

Conflict should not be introduced into games until all players are thoroughly capable of using the focus to create relationships. In the author's early work with children, it became evident that players often used conflict to produce action. Players involved with the focus can connect and interrelate, making physical action possible. If players are absorbed with the story only, conflict is sometimes inevitable. But it is not always necessary. Energy and stage action are generated by the simple process of playing with one another.

□ *If conflict is given too early, involvement will take place between players themselves, creating subjective emotional scenes, verbal battles, even pushing and shoving.*

Role Playing

Many creative dramatics proponents are advocates of role playing in the schoolroom. Role playing when it is used for conflict resolution is best left in the hands of clinical therapists. They are trained to deal with the unearthed emotions and memories that can sometimes arise in participants during role-playing sessions.

For educators who think of role playing as simply an opportunity for young players to take on characters from social studies and literature classes, the Where and Who games are quite useful.

Playing theater games offers all players many chances to experience different points of view and play many parts. But they should not infringe on players' privacy. When players are on focus, they are acting on and out of the moment, experiencing themselves and each other, all present to the moment of playing.

Chapter 20:
REMOVING AMATEUR QUALITIES

Many of us have sat through shows cast with children or nonprofessional adults where, aside from an occasional glimmering of natural charm or a moment of spontaneity, there was little or nothing to redeem the performance. The players might, indeed, have been "expressing themselves," but they were doing so at the expense of the audience. This section sets down some of the so-called "amateurish" qualities in young and inexperienced actors.

The Amateur Actor

1. Has intense stage fright.
2. Does not know what to do with his or her hands.
3. Has awkward stage movements — shifts back and forth, moves aimlessly about stage.
4. Reads lines stiffly, mechanically; forgets lines.
5. Has poor enunciation, rushes speeches.
6. Usually repeats a line he or she has misread.
7. Mouths the words of fellow actors as they are playing.
8. Creates no theater "business."
9. Has no sense of timing.
10. Drops cues, is insensitive to pace.
11. "Emotes" lines instead of talking to fellow actors.
12. "Breaks" on stage.
13. Does not project voice or emotions.
14. Cannot take direction.
15. Hangs on to furniture or props.

Preparing the Player for the Stage

1. Stage fright is fear of judgment. The actor is afraid of criticism, of being ridiculous, of forgetting lines, etc. It can be overcome by a dynamic understanding of the phrases **Share with the audience!** and **Show, don't tell!**

2. Most immature actors use only the mouth and hands. When students learn to act with the whole body (physicalize), the problem of what to do with the hands disappears. In fact, it will never arise after student-actors understand the idea of the focus.

3. Awkward stage movement is usually the result of imposed stage direction. When the actor is trying to re-member instead of allowing stage movement to evolve out of the stage reality, he or she cannot help but move awkwardly. Any object-involvement exercise will help here.

4. Mechanical reading is the result of not creating real-ity. Recitation of the words has become more important to the actor than an understanding of their meaning and relationships. They have remained "words" instead of "dialogue." See Chapters 10 and 11.

5. Poor enunciation and rushed speeches usually result from a lack of understanding on the actor's part that the audience is an integral element of theater.

6. Lines misread and then repeated word for word are examples of rote memorization taking its deadly toll of spontaneity. Training by rote is also the cause of many other amateurish qualities. Meeting a crisis on stage should become second nature to even the youngest actor. Through training, the actor can learn to improvise through any problem of lost or misread dialogue.

7. Mouthing of each other's words is caused by prema-ture memorization, often by allowing young actors to take scripts home, where they memorize everything on the page.

8. The ability to create interesting stage business and blocking can come only from a real understanding of group relationships and involvement.

9. The sense of theater timing can be taught. Timing is recognition of others in the theater reality.

10. Dropped cues and failure to sense pace (like timing) occur when an actor is insensitive to the audience and fellow actors. *All exercises are geared to develop this sen-sitivity.*

11. Declamatory acting or "emoting" results from iso-lation and using the stage subjectively. It is egocentric and exhibitionistic, for the actor is unable to relate the words to fellow actors and thus to the inner feelings which have caused them.

12. When actors "break" or fall out of character on stage, they have lost sight of the internal relationships of the play and their focus.

13. Inadequate projection is caused by fear or neglect of the audience as fellow players.

14. The inability to take direction often stems from a lack of objectivity or inadequate communication between actor and director. The actor may not be free enough yet to meet his or her responsibility to the group. TELEVISION and STORYTELLING give the student a look-in to the director's problems.

15. When the actor moves hesitantly about the stage, clinging from chair to chair, or moves aimlessly about the stage, he or she is showing fear of being exposed to the audience, the central problem of nonprofessional theater. Stressing exercises of group interaction and sharing with the audience will help.

None of the games in this book is designed to eliminate single problems. The effect of the games is cumulative and will solve the above problems and others before they start. After becoming familiar with the games, players will find that the skills, techniques, and spontaneity needed in the theater will fast and forever become their own.

Appendix 1:
WORKSHOP SEQUENCES

(The first of these, with commentary, may be found in Chapter 1. Those following are arranged in order from simplest to most advanced. Where no warm-up game is listed, choose one you like.)

SEQUENCE #2
(Preparing a puppet show)

	Traditional Games (Warm-ups and wrap-ups)	Theater Games
Workshop #1	OBSERVATION GAME* WHO STARTED THE MOTION?*	SENDING SIGHT OUT THREE CHANGES MIRROR WHO IS THE MIRROR?
Workshop #2	RHYTHMIC MOVEMENT OBSERVATION GAME*	SPACE SUBSTANCE PLAY BALL IT'S HEAVIER WHEN IT'S FULL PART OF A WHOLE, OBJECT
Workshop #3	GIVE & TAKE WARM-UP* NAME SIX*	PART OF A WHOLE, ACTIVITY PART OF A WHOLE, OCCUPATION HOW OLD AM I? WHAT DO I DO FOR A LIVING?
Workshop #4	IDENTIFYING OBJECTS* OBJECT MOVES THE PLAYERS*	SPACE SHAPING FOR TEAMS ADD A PART
Workshop #5	POISON*	GIBBERISH INTRODUCTION GIBBERISH/ENGLISH GIBBERISH: TEACHING

Traditional Games (Warm-ups and wrap-ups)	**Theater Games**
Workshop #6	
I See You*	Mirror Follow the Follower Mirror Sound Building a Story
Workshop #7	
When I Go to California* Knocking*	Relating an Incident Adding Color Building a Story
Workshop #8	
	Space Substance Space Shaping (Solo) Relay Where Where Game Playground
Workshop #9	
Give & Take Warm-Up* Adam's Sons*	Feet & Legs Alone #1 Hands Alone (Use sock puppets to illustrate a favorite story. You may want to have players choose characters and decorate their sock puppets to suit their characters.)
Workshop #10	
	Greek Chorus (Use a favorite singing game — Princess Thorn Rosa, Here We Go Round the Mulberry Bush, etc. and illustrate with puppets.) Puppets on Strings

SEQUENCE #3
(Building group spirit)

	Traditional Games (Warm-ups and wrap-ups)	**Theater Games**
Workshop #1	SINGLE FILE* THREE CHANGES* WHO STARTED THE MOTION?*	MIRROR FOLLOW THE FOLLOWER WHO IS THE MIRROR?
Workshop #2	RED LIGHT (CHEESE IT)* NEW YORK (LEMONADE)*	TUG OF WAR JUMP ROPE PLAYGROUND
Workshop #3	SINGING SYLLABLES*	GIBBERISH: TEACHING GIBBERISH/ENGLISH
Workshop #4		FEELING SELF WITH SELF PART OF A WHOLE, ACTIVITY PART OF A WHOLE, OCCUPATION PART OF A WHOLE, OBJECT
Workshop #5		FEELING SELF WITH SELF SEEING THROUGH OBJECTS TOUCH & BE TOUCHED PART OF A WHOLE, RELATIONSHIP WHO AM I?
Workshop #6	EXPLOSION TAG* SLOW MOTION/FREEZE TAG*	RELAY WHERE WHERE GAME WITH DIAGRAMS ADD A PART
Workshop #7 (This may be expanded to several sessions)	GIVE & TAKE WARM-UP*	RELATING AN INCIDENT ADDING COLOR BUILDING A STORY STORYTELLING

Traditional Games (Warm-ups and wrap-ups)	**Theater Games**
Workshop #8	
Poison*	Gibberish Introduction Gibberish/English (See notes on Student Sidecoaching, Chapter 1)
Workshop #9	
Give & Take Warm-Up*	Feet & Legs Alone Hands Alone Total Body Involvement
Workshop #10	
Dumb Crambo*	Box Full of Hats (Storytelling)

SEQUENCE #4
(For experienced players.)
(Warm-up and wrap-up games should be added by the teacher. Many of the workshops include material that may take two, three, or more sessions to cover with your group.)

	Traditional Games (Warm-ups and wrap-ups)	**Theater Games**
Workshop #1	Identifying Objects*	Play Ball Seeing a Sport: Recall How Old Am I?
Workshop #2		What Time Is It? What Do I Do for a Living? Who's Knocking? Observation Game
Workshop #3		Three-Way Conversation
Workshop #4		Follow the Follower Feeling Self with Self Mirror Sound Mirror Speech
Workshop #5	Give & Take Warm-Up*	Handwriting Small Handwriting Blindfolded Handwriting Large Building a Story
Workshop #6		Vocal Sound Effects Soundtrack
Workshop #7	Stage Whisper Warm-Up*	Echo Extended Sound Stage Whisper

	Traditional Games (Warm-ups and wrap-ups)	**Theater Games**
Workshop #8		Follow the Follower Dubbing Charades
Workshop #9		Who Am I? Who Game
Workshop #10		Space Substance Space Shaping for Teams Stage Picture Rocking the Boat/ Sharing the Stage Picture
Workshop #11	Ocean Wave*	What's Beyond: Activity

SEQUENCE #5

	Traditional Games (Warm-ups and wrap-ups)	Theater Games
Workshop #1	SWAT TAG* SINGLE FILE*	FEELING SELF WITH SELF SPACE WALK #1 TOUCH & BE TOUCHED/SEE & BE SEEN (As players move through the space, have each speak out his or her name when passing another player.)
Workshop #2	THREE CHANGES*	SPACE SUBSTANCE SPACE SHAPING (SOLO) PLAYGROUND TUG OF WAR
Workshop #3	NAME SIX*	MIRROR FOLLOW THE FOLLOWER MIRROR SOUND MIRROR SPEECH
Workshop #4	DOG & BONE* WHO STARTED THE MOTION?*	VOCAL SOUND EFFECTS TELEVISION SCREEN
Workshop #5	EXPLOSION TAG* SLOW MOTION/FREEZE TAG* OBSERVATION GAME*	DODGE BALL PLAY BALL
Workshop #6	RED LIGHT (CHEESE IT)*	SPACE SHAPING FOR TEAMS TUG OF WAR PLAYGROUND
Workshop #7	NEW YORK (LEMONADE)*	SPACE WALK #2 (Have players sing out their names as in Workshop #1.) GIBBERISH INTRODUCTION GIBBERISH: SELLING

	Traditional Games (Warm-ups and wrap-ups)	**Theater Games**
Workshop #8		SENDING HEARING OUT GIBBERISH: SELLING (repeat) GIBBERISH/ENGLISH
Workshop #9	STREETS & ALLEYS* STREETS & ALLEYS: VARIATIONS*	RELAY WHERE WHERE GAME
Workshop #10		Where series, Chapter 9
Workshop #11		Who series, Chapter 9
Workshop #12		What series, Chapter 9, or Part of a Whole series, Chapter 7

SEQUENCE #6

Traditional Games (Warm-ups and wrap-ups)	Theater Games

Workshop #1

SLOW MOTION/FREEZE TAG*	MIRROR
THREE CHANGES*	WHO IS THE MIRROR?
	FOLLOW THE FOLLOWER

Workshop #2

| OBJECT RELAY* | FOLLOW THE FOLLOWER |
| NAME SIX* | MIRROR |

Workshop #3

RED LIGHT (CHEESE IT)*	SPACE SUBSTANCE
WHEN I GO TO CALIFORNIA*	PLAY BALL
	PLAYGROUND or JUMP ROPE

Workshop #4

STREETS & ALLEYS*	DODGE BALL
	SPACE SUBSTANCE
	SPACE SHAPING FOR TEAMS
	TUG OF WAR
	INVOLVEMENT WITH LARGE OBJECTS

Workshop #5

	SPACE WALK #1
	TRANSFORMATION OF OBJECTS
	PART OF A WHOLE, ACTIVITY
	PART OF A WHOLE, OCCUPATION
	PART OF A WHOLE, RELATIONSHIP
	WHO AM I?

Workshop #6

	PART OF A WHOLE, OBJECT
	RELAY WHERE
	WHERE GAME WITH DIAGRAMS
	WHERE GAME

	Traditional Games (Warm-ups and wrap-ups)	**Theater Games**
Workshop #7	SINGING SYLLABLES*	GIBBERISH INTRODUCTION GIBBERISH/ENGLISH (Use student sidecoaches)
Workshop #8		THREE-WAY WRITING THREE-WAY CONVERSATION VOWELS & CONSONANTS
Workshop #9		FEELING SELF WITH SELF FOLLOW THE FOLLOWER MIRROR SOUNDS MIRROR SPEECH
Workshop #10	DUMB CRAMBO*	CHARADES DRAWING OBJECTS GAME

SEQUENCE #7

	Traditional Games (Warm-ups and wrap-ups)	Theater Games
Workshop #1	Three Changes* Who Started the Motion?*	Mirror Follow the Follower
Workshop #2		Space Substance Play Ball Dodge Ball Tug of War Playground
Workshop #3	Singing Syllables*	Gibberish Introduction Gibberish: Selling
Workshop #4		Feeling Self with Self Sending Hearing Out Space Walks ##1 & 2 Part of a Whole, Activity Part of a Whole, Occupation Part of a Whole, Object
Workshop #5		Feeling Self with Self Touch & Be Touched Space Walks ##1, 2, and 3 Part of a Whole, Relationship Who Am I?
Workshop #6	Explosion Tag* Slow Motion/Freeze Tag*	Relay Where Where Game with Diagrams Add a Part

Traditional Games (Warm-ups and wrap-ups)	**Theater Games**
Workshop #7	
GIVE & TAKE WARM-UP*	RELATING AN INCIDENT ADDING COLOR BUILDING A STORY (and variations)
Workshop #8	
POISON*	DRAWING OBJECTS GAME GIBBERISH/ENGLISH
Workshop #9	
GIVE & TAKE WARM-UP*	FEET & LEGS ALONE # 2 EXERCISE FOR THE BACK HANDS ALONE (Use sock puppets to begin building stories.)
Workshop #10	
DUMB CRAMBO*	STORYTELLING (Using puppets)

SEQUENCE #8
(A long sequence of brief sessions)

	Traditional Games (Warm-ups and wrap-ups)	Theater Games
Workshop #1		THREE-WAY WRITING (use drawing variation) HOW MUCH DO YOU REMEMBER? THREE-WAY CONVERSATION THREE-WAY WRITING
Workshop #2		MIRROR FOLLOW THE FOLLOWER MIRROR SOUND MIRROR SPEECH
Workshop #3	GIVE & TAKE WARM-UP*	HANDWRITING SMALL HANDWRITING BLINDFOLDED HANDWRITING LARGE BUILDING A STORY
Workshop #4		VOCAL SOUND EFFECTS CHORAL READING
Workshop #5	STAGE WHISPER WARM-UP*	ECHO EXTENDED SOUND STAGE WHISPER
Workshop #6		FOLLOW THE FOLLOWER DUBBING
Workshop #7		TELEVISION SCREEN SHADOW SCREEN (MONTAGE)

	Traditional Games (Warm-ups and wrap-ups)	**Theater Games**
Workshop #8	GIVE & TAKE WARM-UP*	GIVE & TAKE GIVE & TAKE FOR READING
Workshop #9		WHO AM I? WHO GAME SHOWING WHO THROUGH USE OF AN OBJECT CHANGING EMOTION
Workshop #10 (several sessions)		SPACE WALKS ##1, 2, and 3 SPACE WALK BLINDFOLDED
Workshop #11		SPACE SUBSTANCE SPACE SHAPING FOR TEAMS
Workshop #12		STAGE PICTURE
Workshop #13		FOREIGN LANGUAGE GIBBERISH GIBBERISH INTERPRETER
Workshop #14		SINGING SYLLABLES EXTENDED SOUND
Workshop #15		MIRROR SOUND MIRROR SPEECH SEEING THE WORD SPELLING GIVE & TAKE FOR READING

	Traditional Games (Warm-ups and wrap-ups)	**Theater Games**
Workshop #16	QUICK NUMBERS*	CONTACT EYE CONTACT DEAF AUDIENCE PITCHMAN EXITS & ENTRANCES
Workshop #17		WHERE GAME WITH PROPS WHERE WITHOUT HANDS
Workshop #18		EXPLORATION OF A LARGE ENVIRONMENT SHOWING WHERE WITHOUT OBJECTS SPECIALIZED WHERE
Workshop #19		WHERE WITH HELP WHERE WITH OBSTACLES WHERE: HELP/HINDER
Workshop #20		GIVE & TAKE FOR READING SPELLING SEEING THE WORD VERBALIZING THE WHERE ##1 and 2
Workshop #21		SPACE SUBSTANCE TRANSFORMATION OF OBJECTS SPACE WALK #1 SPACE WALK BLINDFOLDED NO MOTION

Appendix 2:
Scope & Sequence of Skills*

Movement

Music & Rhythmic Movement	Energetic Movement	Body Awareness
Elementary Ocean Wave (3) A Walk in the Moonlight (3) Rhythmic Movement (3) I See You (6) Adam's Sons (8) Here We Go Round The Mulberry Bush (9) Isabella (10) Princess Thorn Rosa (10) Poison (14) Skits & Songs (15)	Object Relay (2) Swat Tag (2) Explosion Tag (2) Streets & Alleys (2) Streets & Alleys: Variations (2) Kitty Wants a Corner (10)	Slow Motion/Freeze Tag (3) Feeling Self with Self (4) Tug of War (5) Feet & Legs Alone #1 (13) Hands Alone (13) Total Body Involvement (13) Puppets on Strings (13)
Advanced Ocean Wave (3) Rhythmic Movement (3) Poison (14) *Numbers in parentheses indicate the chapters in which the games are found. Games are categorized by major emphasis and listed in the order in which they appear.	Object Relay (2) Swat Tag (2) Explosion Tag (2) Streets & Alleys (2) Streets & Alleys: Variations (2)	Slow Motion/Freeze Tag (3) No Motion (3) Feeling Self with Self (4) Space Walk #2 (4) Space Walk #3: Skeleton (4) Tug of War (5) Dodge Ball (5) Feet & Legs Alone #1 (13) Feet & Legs Alone #2 (13) Hands Alone (13) Exercise for the Back (13) Total Body Involvement (13) Puppets on Strings (13) Parts of the Body/Full Scene (13)

Scope & Sequence of Skills

Perception & Expression

Observation/Concentration/ Memory	Sensory Awareness	Imitation/Reflection	
Red Light (Cheese It) (2) Single File (6) When I Go to California (6) Three Changes (6) Observation Game (6) Who Started the Motion? (6) Knocking (9) Who's Knocking? (9) Handwriting Large (10) Three-Way Conversation (12)	Touch & Be Touched/ See & Be Seen (4) Sending Sight Out (6) Seeing through Objects (6) Seeing a Sport: Recall (6) Listening to the Environment (6) Dog & Bone (9) Identifying Objects (9) Echo (11) Relating an Incident Adding Color (15)	Mirror (8) Who Is the Mirror? (8) Follow the Follower (8) Mirror Sound (11)	Elementary
Quick Numbers (2) Red Light (Cheese It) (2) Black Magic (6) Egyptian Writing (6) Three Changes (6) Observation Game (6) Who Started the Motion? (6) Handwriting Large (10) Handwriting Small (10) Handwriting Blindfolded (10) How Much Do You Remember? (12) Three-Way Conversation (12) Three-Way Writing (12) Drawing Objects Game (12) Building a Story: Stop Mid-Word (15) Building a Story: Reading (15)	Touch & Be Touched/ See & Be Seen (4) Space Walk #1 (4) Space Walk Blindfolded (4) Sending Sight Out (6) Seeing through Objects (6) Seeing a Sport: Recall (6) Sending Hearing Out (6) Seeing the Word (10) Extended Sound (11) Relating an Incident Adding Color (15)	Mirror (8) Who Is the Mirror? (8) Follow the Follower (8) Mirror Speech (10) Mirror Sound (11) Dubbing (14)	Advanced

Scope & Sequence of Skills

Dramatic Elements

	Setting	Plot	Characterization
Elementary	Where Game with Props (9) Relay Where: Building a Set (9) What Time Is It? (9) Exploration of a Large Environment (9)	Television Screen (14) Shadow Screen (14) Building a Story (15) Storytelling (16)	How Old Am I? (9) What Do I Do for a Living? (9) Who Am I? (9) Who Game (9) Box Full of Hats (15)

Advanced	Where Game with Diagrams (9)
	Where Game with Props (9)
	Relay Where: Building a Set (9)
	Exploration of a
	   Large Environment (9)
	Where without Hands (9)
	Showing Where
	   without Objects (9)
	Where with Help (9)
	Where with Obstacles (9)
	Where: Help/Hinder (9)
	The Specialized Where (9)
		What's Beyond? (9)
		Television Screen (14)
		Shadow Screen (14)
		Building a Story (15)
		Storytelling (16)
			How Old Am I? (9)
			Who Am I? (9)
			Who Game (9)
			Showing Who through
			   Use of an Object (9)
			Box Full of Hats (15)

Scope & Sequence of Skills

Dramatic Elements (cont.)	Teamwork	
Sound & Dialogue	**Role-Playing**	**Collaboration**
Name Six (10) Singing Syllables (10) Gibberish Introduction (11) Gibberish/English (11) Radio (14) Greek Chorus (14) Vocal Sound Effects (14) Choral Reading (14)	Part of a Whole, 　Activity (7) Part of a Whole, 　Occupation (7) Part of a Whole, 　Relationship (7) Airport (9)	Don't Let Go (2) Space Shaping for Teams (5) Jump Rope (5) Involvement with Three 　or More (5) Add a Part (5) Part of a Whole, Object (7) Give & Take Warm-Up (10) Rocking the Boat/ 　Sharing the Stage Picture (19)
Name Six (10) Singing Syllables (10) Gibberish Introduction (11) Gibberish/English (11) Radio (14) Greek Chorus (14) Vocal Sound Effects (14) Soundtrack (14) Choral Reading (14) Spelling (15) Vowels & Consonants (15) Stage Whisper Warm-Up (19) Stage Whisper (19)	Part of a Whole, 　Activity (7) Part of a Whole, 　Occupation (7) Part of a Whole, 　Relationship (7) Airport (9) Give & Take (10)	Don't Let Go (2) Space Shaping for Teams (5) Involvement with Three 　or More (5) Add a Part (5) Part of a Whole, Object (7) Give & Take Warm-Up (10) Give & Take for Reading (10) Stage Picture (19) Rocking the Boat/ 　Sharing the Stage Picture (19)

Elementary

Advanced

Scope & Sequence of Skills

Creativity

	Dramatization	Pantomime	Improvisation

Elementary	Involvement in Twos (5)
	Finding Objects in the
	   Immediate Environment (5)
	It's Heavier When It's Full (5)
	New York (Lemonade) (9)
	Gibberish: Teaching (11)
		Space Substance (5)
		Space Shaping (Solo) (5)
		Play Ball (5)
		Playground (5)
		The Object Moves
		  the Players (5)
		What Am I Eating? Tasting?
		  Smelling? Hearing? (9)
		Involvement with
		  Large Objects (9)
		Involvement without Hands (9)	

Advanced	Involvement in Twos (5)
	Finding Objects in the
	   Immediate Environment (5)
	It's Heavier When It's Full (5)
	Involvement with the
	   Immediate Environment (9)
	Changing Emotion (9)
	Dumb Crambo (10)
	Verbalizing the Where,
	  Part 1 (10)
	Verbalizing the Where,
	  Part 2 (10)
	Gibberish: Selling (11)
	Foreign Language Gibberish
	  (11)
	Gibberish Interpreter (11)
	Charades (15)
	Pitchman (17)
	Deaf Audience (17)
		Space Substance (5)
		Space Shaping (Solo) (5)
		Play Ball (5)
		Playground (5)
		Transformation of Objects (5)
		Difficulty with
		  Small Objects (5)
		The Object Moves
		  the Players (5)
		Involvement with
		  Large Objects (9)
		Involvement without Hands (9)
			Exchanging Wheres (9)
			Where Game (Scene) (9)
			On the Spot (15)
			Eye Contact (17)
			Exits & Entrances (17)
			Contact (19)

Appendix 3:
BIBLIOGRAPHY

A. Supplementary Materials and Teacher Resources

Barlin, Anne Lief. *The Art of Learning through Movement.* Los Angeles: Ward Ritchie Press, 1971. Various kinds of rhythmic movement and gesture are emphasized here. But the development of imagination is the goal of these exercises.

Barnfield, Gabriel. *Creative Drama in the Schools.* London: Macmillan Education Ltd., 1968. Based on experience in Britain, the book provides many good specific suggestions for application in schoolrooms. There are helpful lists of situations, movements to try, and settings to use. There are also good ideas on the use of music and dance for creative drama.

Bauer, Caroline Feller. *Handbook for Storytellers.* Chicago: American Library Association, 1977. Although the emphasis is on storytelling, stories are so often a motivation for creative drama that this book is a valuable and information-packed tool for the classroom teacher. There is a section on creative drama as well in which there are many other good suggestions for developing the senses, using pantomime and beginning improvisation. The book is invaluable for its book lists.

Blackie, Pamela, Bess Bullough, and Doris Nash. *Drama.* New York: Citation Press, 1972. A slim volume of activities for the very young child.

Carlson, Bernice Wells. *Let's Pretend It Happened to You.* Nashville: Abingdon Press, 1973. This book contains stories and dramatic extensions plus a general overview of how to use creative drama with groups of younger children. It provides material on opening activities, story sharing, discussion and planning, playing the story, and evaluation. A good beginning resource.

Chambers, Dewey. *Storytelling and Creative Drama.* Dubuque, Iowa: William C. Brown, 1970. Very clear description of how to help children dramatize a story. The classroom teacher may wish to reduce the planning stage, but the basic principles presented are sound and there are many good specific suggestions for the classroom teacher. The book will also be helpful to the teacher who wishes to tell rather than read a story before dramatic activity begins.

Cheifitz, Dan. *Theatre in My Head.* Boston: Little, Brown & Co., 1971. Useful primarily for background and understanding. The book is a description of one practitioner's work with a group of inner-city eight- to eleven-year-olds.

Cranston, Jerneal. *Dramatic Imagination.* Eureka, California: Interface California Corporation, 1975. Exercises for the senses and the imagination, a good overview of creative dramatics, and many stories nicely opened out for drama by this experienced teacher. There are more than one hundred well-explained exercises and twenty fully developed lesson plans, many of which can be integrated with what is happening in the curriculum.

Cullum, Albert. *Push Back the Desks.* New York: Citation Press, 1967. Useful primarily for background and understanding. The book touches on creative drama as well as other creative approaches for getting children involved. More a narrative than a hands-on, how-to book.

Gilbert, Anne Green. *Teaching the Three R's through Movement Experiences.* Minneapolis, Minnesota: Burgess Publishing Co., 1977. Although some of the exercises may lose dramatic impact in an effort to make them relate to curriculum, there are many useful short classroom exercises. These are transitional, warm-up, or motivational activities rather than whole lesson plans. There is not enough here on which to build a creative drama program, but the book contains useful supplemental material.

Heinig, Ruth and Lyda Stillwell. *Creative Drama for the Classroom Teacher.* Englewood Cliffs, N.J.: Prentice-Hall, 1981. A comprehensive sourcebook for developing a creative drama program in the classroom. Covers everything from simple activities like games to pantomime, creating dialogue in scenes, and story dramatization. Excellent bibliography.

Hodgson, John and Ernest Richards. *Improvisation.* New York: Grove Press, 1974. Many practical suggestions with examples of how to use improvisation with and without a text to help students become more responsive, expressive, and facile with language.

Jennings, Sue. *Remedial Drama.* New York: Theatre Arts, 1974. Although focused on drama with the handicapped, this sensitive exploration of creative drama has many applications for any group. The book is a description and anecdotal record of the author's own experience, rather than a hands-on teaching tool, but it provides excellent background.

Kelly, Elizabeth Y. *The Magic If: Stanislavski for Children.* Baltimore: National Educational Press, 1973. Oriented towards performance, this book provides many imaginative exercises to be used within a creative drama context. There is good material for developing awareness and imagination, concentration, the senses, and communication.

Keysell, Pat. *Motives for Mime.* London: Evans Brothers, Ltd., 1975. Keysell goes beyond mime to include many good imagination stretchers and internal control building exercises, sequentially laid out from the simplest to the most difficult. Easy to understand and use.

Lazarus, Joan. *Theatre Arts Discoveries: A Leader's Guide to Informal Drama Activities.* Madison, Wisconsin: Department of Continuing Education in the Arts, University of Wisconsin – Madison, 1986. This useful publication is designed as a guide for leaders with no formal drama training. It uses a learning-by-doing workbook approach and walks leaders step by step through the

assessment of their group's present skills, the planning
of creative drama activities, and leading sessions. There
is an extensive resources section including sample lesson plans, ideas for improvisation, and suggestions for
story drama. Companion video tapes are available.

Lowndes, Betty. *Movement and Creative Drama for Children.* Boston, Mass.: Plays, Inc. A collection of exercises
and theater games developed in English primary
schools. The book emphasizes sensory awareness and
mimetic movement but there is also some discussion
of the psychological development of young children.

McCaslin, Nellie. *Act Now! Plays and Ways to Make
Them.* New York: S. G. Phillips, 1975. Though not directed toward creative drama, this book contains many
good warm-up exercises and games as well as ideas for
playmaking. It will be especially useful for the classroom teacher who wants to help children prepare a play
for performance. There are ideas for lighting, props,
scenery, make-up, costumes, puppets, and scripting
your own play.

———, ed. *Children and Drama.* New York: David
McKay, 1975. An anthology by many experts in the
field. A theoretical rather than practical book, this provides the classroom teacher with a good overview and
understanding of what creative drama is and why it is
important.

———. *Creative Drama in the Classroom.* New York:
Longman, Inc., 1984. A helpful book full of practical
suggestions for how to make creative drama work in
the classroom for you. There is material on movement,
imagination, and improvisation, and an emphasis on
how to make plays. The annotated bibliography is also
valuable.

Rosenberg, Helene S. and Patricia Pinciotti. *Creative
Drama and Imagination: Transforming Ideas into Action.* New York: Holt, Rinehart & Winston, 1986. This
comprehensive book begins with a presentation of the
basic elements of creative drama and provides a com-

plete yet succinct overview accompanied by beautiful illustrations. The second half contains a series of activities and outlines the imagination-in-action format.

Scher, Anna and Charles Veral. *One Hundred Plus Ideas for Drama.* London: Heinemann Educational Books, 1981. A very practical book by an experienced English drama leader. Concise, straightforward descriptions of games, verbal exercises, warm-ups, mime, and movement, as well as helpful tips on concentration, participant self-discipline, and group management.

Schwartz, Dorothy and Dorothy Aldrich, eds. *Give Them Roots and Wings.* Washington, D.C.: American Theatre Association, 1972. Easy-to-follow creative drama lessons prepared by leaders in the creative drama field. There are activities that deal with movement and pantomime, sensitivity, characterization, improvisation, dialogue and vocalization, and dramatic form as well as an introductory discussion of why creative drama is important.

Siks, Geraldine Brain. *Drama with Children.* 2nd ed. New York: Harper & Row, 1983. This provides the classroom teacher with a good understanding of the elements of creative drama, the skills children will be developing, and the value of such work to the curriculum. There are many specific activities and examples based on a lifetime of experience and presented in a logical developmental sequence. Best if referred to after some exposure to the philosophy and practice of creative drama.

Siks, Geraldine and Hazel Brain Dunnington, eds. *Children's Theatre and Creative Dramatics.* Seattle: University of Washington Press, 1961. An eclectic collection of articles on children's theater and creative drama by leaders in the field. Although it is probably of limited value for newcomers, it will be a valuable reference to those who want to learn more and dig deeper.

Sills, Paul. *Story Theater.* New York: Samuel French, Inc., 1971. These plays may be too difficult for children. But they provide the best possible examples of fairy tales and legends translated into performance. This collection, performed in New York at the beginning of the 1970s, was a huge success.

Spolin, Viola. *Improvisation for the Theater.* Evanston, Ill.: Northwestern University Press, 1963. The most comprehensive book to date on improvisation. Many of the exercises included can be used in the classroom with older children to build concentration and communications skills. A special section is devoted to children's theater.

———. *The Theater Game File.* St. Louis: Cemrel, Inc., 1975. Theater games on cards rather than in bound book form.

———. *Theater Games for Rehearsal.* Evanston, Ill.: Northwestern University Press, 1985. Clear directions for improvisational games that build skill and concentration. Each game includes a well-defined purpose and focus, complete description, and suggested sidecoaching and evaluation comments. The book is intended for groups planning productions, but is also valuable for all those interested in theater games.

Stewig, John. *Informal Drama in the Elementary Language Arts Program.* New York: Teachers College Press, 1983. This enormously helpful book does a good job of explaining the what, why, and how of creative drama as well as laying out a sequential approach that can be readily applied by the classroom teacher. The book is clearly written and abounds in illustrative detail.

———. *Spontaneous Drama: A Language Art.* Columbus, Ohio: Charles E. Merrill, 1973. Helpful guide to the classroom teacher who wishes to use creative drama as a language art. Good examples from an educator who knows children and creative drama well. Stewig provides a helpful approach to spontaneous drama experiences which include developing material, discussion-questioning segments, and evaluation.

Tynas, Bill. *Child Drama in Action (A Practical Manual for Teachers)*. Toronto, Ontario: Gage Educational Publishing, 1971. Some good do's and don't's and a ready-made approach for the beginner.. The teacher may soon wish to depart from the script and add ideas of his or her own as they evolve. Some directions may need modifying to avoid bedlam, but there are many good ideas nevertheless, particularly for teachers of older children.

Wagner, Betty Jane. *Dorothy Heathcote (Drama as a Learning Medium)*. Washington, D.C.: National Education Association, 1976. A description of the work of the great English teacher. It might be difficult for those inexperienced in creative drama to put Heathcote's approach to work in the classroom, but elements of it can be used to enhance conceptual understanding and problem solving. The philosophy stresses "you are there" situations in which students "become" various characters in history, literature, or modern-day life and reflect on their experiences.

Ward, Winifred. *Playmaking with Children from Kindergarten to High School*. New York: Appleton-Century-Crofts, 1957. A classic in children's drama, with particular emphasis on storytelling by one of the great teachers in this field. See also Ward's *Creative Drama with and for Children*, Washington: Office of Education, 1960, and *Stories to Dramatize*, Anchorage, Ky.: Anchorage Press, 1957.

Way, Brian. *Development through Drama*. Atlantic Highlands, N.J.: Humanities Press, 1972. An excellent introduction to what creative drama is and what it can do for the whole child. There are many ideas to try, but even more, the book provides the classroom teacher with a good foundation to build on.

Whittam, Penny. *Teaching Speech and Drama in the Infant School*. London: Ward Lock Educational, 1977. Clear lesson plans and tie-ins to classroom curriculum, stories and poems to dramatize, and much practical information.

Zavatsky, Bill, and Ron Padgett, eds. *The Whole Word Catalogue 2.* New York: McGraw-Hill, 1977. While this collection of essays is by and for teachers of writing, it is an excellent approach to the stimulating of creativity in children.

Ziskind, Sylvia. *Telling Stories to Children.* New York: H. W. Wilson Co., 1976. A good, straightforward survey of storytelling techniques, with fine examples of adaptable stories.

B. A Short List of Good Books on Puppetry

Baird, Bil. *Art of the Puppet.* Boston: Plays, Inc., 1966.

Batchelder, Marjorie. *The Puppet Theater Handbook.* New York: Harper & Brothers, 1947.

Cole, Nancy. *Puppet Theatre in Performance.* New York: Wm. Morrow, 1978.

Cummings, Richard. *101 Hand Puppets.* New York: McKay, 1962.

Hanford, Robert Ten Eyck. *The Complete Book of Puppets and Puppeteering.* New York and London: Drake, 1976.

Jenkins, Peggy Davison. *The Magic of Puppetry.* Englewood Cliffs, N.J.: Prentice-Hall, Inc., 1980.

Peyton, Jeffrey, and Barbara Koenig. *Puppetry: A Tool for Teaching.* New Haven: P.O. Box 270, 1973.

McCaslin, Nellie. *Puppet Fun.* New York: McKay, 1977.

Ross, Laura. *Puppet Shows Using Poems and Stories.* New York: Lothrop, Lee & Shepard, 1970.

C. Stories, Legends, Fables, and Games

Aesop. *Fables of Aesop.* New York: Penguin, 1964. The great fables are deceptively complex. Older players, able to plumb the complexities of animal (and human) behavior, will enjoy using them as the basis of performance pieces. Any edition will do.

Andersen, Hans Christian. *The Nightingale.* New York: Harper & Row, 1965. An emperor discovers that the "real thing" is much more important than a gilded imitation. Parts for everyone as courtiers or townspeople.

Asbjornsen, Peter C., and Jorgen E. Moe. *The Three Billy Goats Gruff.* New York: Harcourt Brace Jovanovich, 1957. The classic story gives rise to many possibilities for movement as all children become the goats, the trees and grass, the river, etc.

Blake, William. *Songs of Innocence and of Experience.* Any edition. The language of most of these and the sentiments of a few may make the poems inaccessible. But some poems, "Laughing Song," "Spring," "The Tyger," will be fascinating to older students.

Boyd, Neva L. *Handbook of Games.* New York: Dover Publications, 1975. The most available source of Boyd's life-long work collecting and formulating folk games.

Brown, Marcia. *Stone Soup.* New York: Scribner's, 1947. To think! The soldiers can make soup from stones. Children enjoy hearing this delightful tale and "becoming" the peasants and soldiers.

Bulfinch, Thomas. *Bulfinch's Mythology.* 2d rev. ed. New York: T. Y. Crowell, 1970. Adventures and excitement abound in this collection. Other editions will do as well.

Carle, Eric. *The Very Hungry Caterpillar.* New York: World Pub. Co., 1972. Wonderful for very young children as they explore movement and nature.

Childcraft. *The How and Why Library: Stories and Fables.* Chicago: Worldbook-Childcraft International, Inc., 1979. A wealth of material from animal tales to fables to fairy tales and more.

Courlander, Harold. *The Hat Shaking Dance and Other Ashanti Tales from Ghana.* New York: Harcourt Brace Jovanovich, 1957. Anansi, the spider, that trickster, is always found out in the end, but meanwhile his merry pranks provide many opportunities for characterization as children "become" animals in the jungle.

———. *The King's Drum.* New York: Harcourt Brace Jovanovich, 1970. This collection of sub-Saharan tales — many about animals — has some funny moments. Particularly wonderful is the title story.

———. *A Treasury of African Folklore.* New York: Crown Publishers, 1975. Courlander's most comprehensive collection of African tales.

De Paola, Tomie. *The Clown of God.* San Diego: Harcourt Brace Jovanovich, 1978. This sensitive tale about the best gift of all, the gift of sincere love, provides food for thought as well as material for dramatization. Many other De Paola books also provide useful material.

Grimm, Jacob and Wilhelm. *The Fisherman and His Wife.* New York: Greenwillow, 1979. Playing the characters in this story provides much opportunity for facial and vocal expression. The fisherman's wife just doesn't know when to stop asking for more.

———. *The Seven Ravens.* New York: Harcourt Brace Jovanovich, 1962. This tale provides possibilities for movement and meaning as the princess searches for her seven lost brothers who have been turned into ravens.

Hatch, Mary C. *Thirteen Danish Tales.* New York: Harcourt, 1947. Humor and stories that are begging to be dramatized. From the young lad who tries to sell butter to a stone to the best detective in the whole world, students will be captivated.

Johnson, Edna, Evelyn R. Sickels, and Frances Clarke Sayers. *Anthology of Children's Literature.* Boston: Houghton Mifflin, 1970. Indian legends, folklore, classic tales, and more provide months and months of material for any classroom. Especially good Indian legends tell of how the Pleiades got to the sky, the coyote who danced with the blackbirds, and how the crow's tail got to be that way.

Lear, Edward. *Book of Nonsense.* New York: Dutton, 1976. Lear was arguably as great a children's writer as Lewis Carroll and he is certainly funnier. Some of his middle-length poems ("Two Old Bachelors," "The Daddy Long-Legs and the Fly," "The Nutcrackers and the Sugar-Tongs," "The Owl and the Pussycat") are possible performance pieces.

Manning-Sanders, Ruth. *A Book of Ogres and Trolls.* New York: Dutton, 1973. Adventure abounds as Nils meets up with a giant troll in the forest and Karl cannot find his cow. These stories are excellent for dramatization and outstanding as motivators for creative writing.

Marriott, Alice. *Saynday's People.* University of Nebraska Press, 1973. A collection about the sympathetic Kiowa hero, Saynday.

———. *Winter Telling Stories.* New York: Wm. Sloane, 1947. Of Marriott's several collections of American Indian stories, this is probably the most useful in providing material for storytelling.

Minard, Rosemary, *Womenfolk and Fairy Tales.* Boston: Houghton Mifflin Co., 1975. A collection of women in fairy tales, from the Three Chinese Red Riding Hoods to the woman who flummoxed the fairies. Children can't wait to perform these stories.

Sendak, Maurice. *Where the Wild Things Are.* New York: Harper & Row, 1963. Movement, facial expression, sound, characterization, and more spring easily from a sharing of this well-loved picture book.

Seuss, Dr. *The 500 Hats of Bartholomew Cubbins.* New York: Vanguard, 1938. Movement, humor, and possibilities for playmaking abound as each hat removed is replaced in the wink of an eye.

Stern, James, ed. *The Complete Grimm's Fairy Tales.* New York: Pantheon, 1972. A good and relatively recent collection of one of the best resources for story theater. Any reasonably authentic collection of Grimm tales is invaluable.

Thurber, James. *Fables for Our Time & Famous Poems.* New York: Harper & Row, 1974. These funny moral tales are written for adults, but on a certain level they are right for children also.

———. *Many Moons.* New York: Harcourt, 1943. Everyone can join the court in trying to discover how to cheer the princess up.

Uchida, Yoshiko. *The Magic Listening Cap.* New York: Harcourt Brace Jovanovich, 1965. Excellent stories for dramatization and for exploring puppetry and shadow effects.

Viorst, Judith. *Alexander and the Terrible, Horrible, No Good, Very Bad Day.* New York: Atheneum, 1972. Everybody's had one and what fun to relate to such a day in drama.

A fine resource for folk tales, literature, drama, music, and supplementary curriculum material is the Children's Book and Music Center. A catalog is available: Children's Book and Music Center, Post Office Box 1130, Santa Monica, California 90406.

D. Poetry, Writing, and Storytelling

Baldwin, Frances and Margaret Whitehead. *That Way & This.* London: Chatto & Windus, 1972. Poems that foster movement.

Blishen, Edward. *Oxford Book of Poetry for Children.* Danbury, Conn.: Franklin Watts, Inc., 1963. A comprehensive anthology.

Childcraft. *The How and Why Library: Poems and Rhymes.* Chicago: Worldbook-Childcraft International, Inc., 1979. A wealth of material to foster thought, movement, and expression.

Jackson, Jacqueline. *Turn Not Pale, Beloved Snail.* Boston: Little, Brown, 1974. "A book about writing and other things."

Koch, Kenneth. *Wishes, Lies and Dreams.* New York: Chelsea House Publishers, 1970. Teaching the writing of poetry to children.

Lewis, Richard, ed. *Miracles.* New York: Simon & Schuster, 1966. Poems by English-speaking children around the world.

Lueders, Edward and Primus St. John, eds. *Zero Makes Me Hungry.* New York: Scott Foresman, 1976.

McDermott, Beverly Brodsky. *The Crystal Apple.* New York: Viking, 1974. A Russian tale about a girl and her powerful imagination.

Opie, Iona and Peter. *Oxford Book of Children's Verse.* Oxford: Oxford University Press, 1973.

Silverstein, Shel. *A Light in the Attic.* New York: Harper & Row, 1981. Zany verses that chidren can relate to and make their own through improvisation.

Stevenson, Robert Louis. *A Child's Garden of Verses.* Any edition. Many of these poems are performable. And understanding them is certainly enhanced by students who have "opened them out" through performance.

Appendix 4:
INDEXES OF GAMES

Alphabetical Index

B. Games Cross-referenced by Curriculum Area

Many of the games included here are useful in teaching topics in other areas of the curriculum. The following games, however, specifically refer to subjects in general science, social studies, and other areas. Use them as examples of ways to adapt theater games to other fields of inquiry.

General Science and Environmental Studies

Social Studies, History, and Consumer Education

Theater

Radio, TV, Film

Literature and Writing

Appendix 5:
GLOSSARY

(Terms italicized below are specifically, though not exclusively, part of the theater-games vocabulary.)

Aside. An observation or remark made by an actor to the audience that is accepted as being not heard by the other characters.

Avant-garde theater. Experimental theater that attempts to break new ground. This kind of theater may abandon many of the traditional theatrical elements.

Backstage. The area, typically behind the stage, where the dressing rooms are and where props and set pieces are kept until needed.

Beat. The smallest (and most natural) unit of a scene. A section of a play in which one character leads or dominates or in which one idea is expressed.

Blocking. The pattern actors follow in moving around on stage. Usually determined by the director; when created by the actor, this is called "self-blocking."

Bunraku. Japanese puppet theater, based on Kabuki plays.

Casting. Selecting which actors will play which roles.

Character. One of the people who figures in a play; a part played by an actor.

Climax. The point of most interest, excitement, or tension in a play. Often, the turning point in the action.

Comedy. Generally used to mean a funny play. However, in classical terms, a comedy is any play with a happy ending and, therefore, may refer to almost any play other than a tragedy.

Commedia dell'arte. First developed during the sixteenth century in Italy, this is improvisational theater in which the actors wear masks.

Conflict. The struggle between opposing ideas, interests, or forces in a play. The existence of conflict, either external or internal — within a character — is central to drama.

Convention. Any familiar theatrical custom that is accepted unquestioningly by the audience. See **Aside**, as an example.

Dialogue. The words spoken by actors during a play. Typically used to mean conversation between characters, but can mean any talking in a play.

Downstage, upstage. Downstage is the part of the stage closest to the audience; upstage is the part farthest away. The terms come from the raked stages of the nineteenth century and earlier, on which upstage was much higher than downstage, thus improving sightlines.

Farce. An exaggerated comedy based on broadly humorous, usually stock, situations and physical (slapstick) jokes.

Focus. A problem at the center of a game which players must resolve. A point of concentration for the players.

Greek theater. Generally used to mean the theater that developed in ancient Greece during the fifth century, B.C. The most famous writers are Aeschylus, Sophocles, Euripides, and Aristophanes.

Hand prop. See **Property.**

Kabuki theater. National theater of Japan (along with Noh drama, which predates it), utilizing stylized make-up and scenery and elaborate costumes.

Marionette. A doll that moves when strings or wires attached to its limbs and head are moved. The term comes from French dolls called "little Marys."

Melodrama. A type of play in which the plot is highly suspenseful and involves a conflict between good characters and evil ones. The term is frequently used to criticize simplistic plotting, one-dimensional characters, and coarse acting.

Method acting. Acting according to the idea that the actor must understand, through his or her own personal experience, the entire life and psychological make-up of the character whose role he or she is portraying. In method acting, an actor portraying a loner would isolate himself or herself during offstage life to prepare for the role. This method was developed and taught by Konstantin Stanislavski and perpetuated by the Moscow Art Theater and, in New York, by the Actors Studio.

Mime. Stylized pantomime; more exaggerated than true pantomime. Often performed today in black clothing and white make-up.

Mirror reflection. Noncerebral response to the action of another player.

Noh drama. Classical Japanese theater, essentially unchanged since the Middle Ages. Noh drama is performed without scenery (except for one tree) and is accompanied by traditional music.

Pantomime. A scene or play without words. The actors use only action and gesture to express their meaning.

Plot. What happens in a play; the sequence of events.

Property, or **prop.** An object used by actors on stage during a play. A table that is moved in for some scenes only is a prop. A **hand prop** is something small enough to be carried — a coffee pot, for example.

Renaissance theater. The theater that developed in England during the reigns of Queen Elizabeth I and King James I. Its leading lights were Marlowe, Shakespeare, Jonson, and Beaumont and Fletcher.

Role. A part as written by the playwright. The basis of an actor's characterization.

Set. The scenery and furniture used during a play. A **set piece** is any individual item, such as a sofa.

Sightlines. The straight lines between the actors on stage and all the members of an audience. If members of an audience must peek around pillars, say, to see stage action, a theater is said to have poor sightlines.

Space object. An object made of space, a projection of players into the physical world.

Space walk. A type of exercise used to help players fully perceive their environment.

Stage business. Actions or behavior, usually created by the actor, used to clarify characterization or create atmosphere. Juggling boiled eggs at the breakfast table would be an example of stage business, if it was not a direction given in the play, although most stage business, such as drumming one's fingers nervously, is less dramatic.

Stage left, stage right, center stage. Directions relative to the actor's vantage point while facing the audience. Stage left, therefore, is to the actor's left and the audience's right.

Stage picture. The succession of tableaux created by a director through blocking.

Tragedy. A play involving suffering and frequently death for the main character, usually caused by a "tragic flaw" in his or her nature. In classical Greek theater, a character's suffering was intended to teach and purify the audience.

What. Stage action. It should not be confused with plot.

Where. Environment, whether on stage or in the outside world.

Who. Character and relationships as shown through behavior.